Praise for Organize Tomorrow Today

"Positive, upbeat . . . actionable, attainable . . . entertaining and readable . . . Put into practice, the skills outlined in this book can be life-changing, and get you to the level of performance you crave."

—SAN FRANCISCO BOOK REVIEW

"*Organize Tomorrow Today* helped me increase my business over 30 percent in six months and, most importantly, improved my balance at home. Small disciplines practiced every day equal success! It's a must read for high achievers."

—VICKIE WICKS, General Partner, Edward Jones

"Dr. Jason Selk and Tom Bartow are experts at peak performance and productivity. In this book they not only teach you what to do, they teach you how to think. And that may be the difference between just knowing and succeeding."

—SHEP HYKEN, *New York Times* bestselling
business author of *The Amazement Revolution*

"An outstanding read. I only wish it had been around earlier in my career."

—DAVE SHORT, former Chairman and CEO of American Funds

"The concepts in *Organize Tomorrow Today* can be used on the playing field and in the board room. Jason and Tom 'nail it' by showing all of us that self-improvement is a process and not an event. I've known both of these individuals for some time now and they both walk the walk."

—TOM ERICKSON, Partner, KPMG

Organize Tomorrow Today

Organize
Tomorrow
T☑DAY

8 Ways to Retrain Your Mind
to Optimize Performance at Work and in Life

Dr. Jason Selk + Tom Bartow
with Matthew Rudy

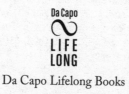

Da Capo Lifelong Books

Designed by Trish Wilkinson
Set in 11-point Adobe Caslon Pro by Perseus Books

Library of Congress Cataloging-in-Publication Data

Selk, Jason, author.
    Organize tomorrow today : 8 ways to retrain your mind to optimize performance at work and in life / Dr. Jason Selk and Tom Bartow, with Matthew Rudy.
        pages   cm
    Includes bibliographical references and index.
    ISBN 978-0-7382-1869-4 (hardback) — ISBN 978-0-7382-1870-0 (e-book)
1. Time management. 2. Habit. 3. Performance. I. Bartow, Tom, author.
II. Rudy, Matthew, author. III. Title.
BF637.T5S45 2015
158—dc23   2015025600

First Da Capo Press hardcover edition 2015
First Da Capo Press paperback edition 2016
ISBN: 978-0-7382-1953-0 (paperback)

Published by Da Capo Press
an imprint of Perseus Books, LLC, a subsidiary of Hachette Book Group, Inc.
www.dacapopress.com

Da Capo Press books are available at special discounts for bulk purchases in the U.S. by corporations, institutions, and other organizations. For more information, please contact the Special Markets Department at Perseus Books, 2300 Chestnut Street, Suite 200, Philadelphia, PA, 19103, or call (800) 810-4145, ext. 5000, or email special.markets@perseusbooks.com.

LSC - C
10 9 8 7 6 5 4

This book is dedicated to
everyone out there trying to improve.
No matter what the outcome, you never embarrass
yourself by emphasizing improvement.

It is the effort to improve that is valuable. By repeating it over and over you will master it.

—SHUNRYU SUZUKI

Contents

Foreword

When I speak to people about my dad, Coach John Wooden, one of the first things they usually want to know is what he was like in the "real world," outside of what you saw at a basketball game.

Dad was a simple, consistent person, who developed and lived by a core set of principles his entire life. He wasn't a brimstone preacher—either inside the locker room or at our house. He was a motivator in a different way—by being a true teacher, and not "just" a coach.

Over the years, his players and the other people he met through basketball came to understand very well that Dad's philosophies and approach weren't some sort of program that he followed some of the time, or "put on" to look better in the media or in recruiting.

He talked about what he believed. He followed it. And he never stopped thinking about ways to make small improvements. He was always teaching, but he was also always learning.

Basketball was very important to my dad, but the core beliefs and philosophies he had—many of which Jason and Tom talk about in this book—aren't about basketball.

They're about life.

It always amazed Dad that he became more famous in retirement than he ever was as an active coach. But I think that fame came for exactly those reasons. People began to understand that those principles applied to far more than basketball—especially in the business world.

In the last two and a half years of Dad's life, I was fortunate to be able to spend two days of every week with him. It was the best time in my life. So many of the friends he made in and outside of basketball would come by, and he stayed connected to the game.

The talks he was able to give in corporate America through people like Tom really brought him a lot of joy. It wasn't about the money he could make. It was about getting his core message through to people young in life—the pyramid of success, the two sets of three, making friendship a fine art.

I heard him say those same things for fifty years, but they weren't just catchphrases. They're the basic building blocks of a life well lived. I used the same principles with my own kids, and now they're using them with their own children.

When we're shooting hoops, my grandson—John Wooden's great-great grandson—will use the backboard on a shot and say, "That's what Paw-Paw wanted me to do."

Dad would have been thrilled to know he influenced Tom and Jason to go out and help so many people in the business and sports worlds.

Jim Wooden
June 15, 2015

Introduction
Sports Psychology Meets Wall Street

"YOU HAVE TEN MINUTES . . . "

Jason Selk was standing in the St. Louis Cardinals' clubhouse at their spring training facility in Jupiter, Florida, in March 2006, getting ready for what he had originally thought was going to be a two-hour introductory presentation in his new role as the Cardinals' director of mental training.

Cardinals general manager Walt Jocketty had extended the invitation to Jason before the season, but when he brought him into manager Tony La Russa's office in the clubhouse, it was clear that what Jason had was an audition—not a job.

After Jason gave a brief synopsis of the two hours of material he had prepared, La Russa looked up from the paperwork on his desk.

"You have ten minutes."

Moments later, looking out at that clubhouse full of All-Stars and future Hall-of-Famers—guys like La Russa, Albert Pujols, Chris Carpenter, and Scott Rolen—Jason decided to introduce his Mental Workout concept. The full version of the workout is designed for elite athletes, and it involves visualization, positive self-talk, and controlled breathing.

After Jason worked through the first step of the Mental Workout, pitching coach Dave Duncan asked to go through the second step. Jason was up against the time limit, so he looked over to Tony to see if it was okay to continue. He nodded, and Jason shared the second step.

When he finished, All-Star third baseman Scott Rolen chimed in and asked if he could share the third step. Again, Jason got the okay from Tony to continue.

After Jason shared the third step, reigning Cy Young Award winner Chris Carpenter stopped him and got up. "Everybody better pay attention," he said. "This is what we need to take it to the next level."

From that moment, Jason was accepted as part of the staff, and he built some incredible relationships with the players over the next six seasons. At the top of any professional sport, the physical differences between the teams are minuscule. The smallest mental edge can mean the difference between losing in the National League Division Series and holding up the World Series trophy. Those Cardinals teams won three division titles and two World Series championships, and at least a small part of that success came from the peak mental performance training the team got from Jason.

Working with the Cardinals certainly helped confirm Jason's credentials in the world of sports psychology and open a lot of doors. But he got something much more valuable than a professional credential or some references out of the experience.

As he was giving that first talk in the clubhouse in March 2006, the Cardinals staff and players didn't know much about him. They didn't know if he had something useful to offer. But he wasn't more than a few minutes into his talk when he noticed that the majority of the players and coaches were taking notes.

The Cardinals have long been considered one of the model franchises in all of professional sports, and at that moment some of the whys behind that reputation became crystal clear to Jason.

From the top down, they established an "obsession for improvement" as a key part of their culture. No matter how successful they got, they were always on the lookout for new information that could help them improve—and a better program for incorporating that information in an organized, efficient way.

Organize Tomorrow Today is that program.

It is a guide for using your most powerful (and often most underestimated) tool—your mind—the way it was designed to be used.

OVERLOAD

Modern life can demand an almost overwhelming amount of attention.

It isn't any surprise that a huge "time management" industry has grown up around this reality. Amazon is stuffed with books—and devices—designed to do everything from manage your schedule to convert you to a paperless office. A thousand different calendar and schedule apps will turn your smartphone into a battery-powered personal assistant—one that works twenty-four hours a day.

There's one problem.

Nobody fully understands the power of the mind. It is an incredibly powerful thing—and one we constantly underestimate. But it wasn't designed to function that way.

In 1956, Dr. George Miller published one of the most influential papers in the history of psychology. He called it "The Magical

Number Seven, Plus or Minus Two," and it outlined for the first time a human's mental "channel capacity"—the amount of information the average person could remember at a given time.[1] It wasn't so clear-cut as the title, but Miller's basic premise is still valid—so much so that it's referred to as Miller's Law. Humans can only process up to seven simple concepts at a given time. This channel-capacity law actually serves as the underpinning of the modern phone-number system. Seven numbers are the most people can easily remember.

What happens when we flood our brains with information?

Once we start thinking about more than a handful of things at a time, our ability to execute *any* of those things at a high level becomes compromised. And the problem is compounded by the fact that very few of the things we're asking our minds to do are simple or one-dimensional, like remembering the digit of a phone number. We're asking our minds to tackle multiple multidimensional tasks at one time—and our channel capacity at that level falls short. We can't really carry in our "working memory" any more than *three* things at one time and have a chance of doing any of them well.

It's something like being a beginner juggler. If you work at it, you can handle juggling three things at once. But once a fourth item gets thrown in, the system is overloaded and it all gets dropped.

George Miller found all of this to be true in the 1950s—when nobody was carrying around high-powered miniature computers in their pockets, mail came in an envelope with a stamp on it, and "twitter" was just something the birds did.

Today, his findings are more valid than ever. All of us are busier than ever before. It's way more than just work: We're making calls, sending texts, going to meetings (real and virtual), and "networking" with professional colleagues. We're wrestling to balance work and home life in a time when information doesn't operate on a "normal" 9-to-5 schedule.

The best time management plan in the world—or the best calendar, or the best device, or the best app—doesn't address the fundamental problem of channel capacity. If technology were the answer, success would be as simple as flipping a switch.

Figuring out how to hack Miller's Law and find more mental bandwidth isn't going to help you live a more productive life. Fitting more pieces into the puzzle won't make you more successful.

In *Organize Tomorrow Today*, we're going to show you how to embrace channel capacity instead of fighting against it. You're going to learn how to make decisions, establish priorities, and light your own motivating fire instead of continuing to chase the counterintuitive concept of multitasking. Most people still seem to believe that being busy is the equivalent of being important, but the highly successful have learned that being busy is a waste of time: being productive is the goal.

WHY SELK AND BARTOW?

Dr. Jason Selk has been training world-class athletes for peak mental performance for almost two decades, including that six-year stint as the St. Louis Cardinals' mental performance coach. Those Cardinal teams won two Worlds Series titles in that span. He has worked with Olympians and professional athletes in every major sport, including the NFL, NBA, Major League Baseball, the PGA and LPGA tours, NASCAR, and the Ultimate Fighting Championships. Jason has written two other groundbreaking mental performance books—*10-Minute Toughness* and *Executive Toughness*. His work has appeared in dozens of magazines, from *Men's Health* to *Shape*, and he has appeared on numerous television shows for major networks and cable channels like ESPN, NBC, and CBS.

Tom Bartow essentially rewrote the book on how to train financial advisors. His concepts have been used by tens of thousands of them, first at Edward Jones—where Tom created that company's top-rated Advanced Training Program—and then at American Funds Group. On the Friday after the September 11 tragedies in 2001, American Funds chairman Dave Short and Tom devised the company's business plan to move forward in the uncertain markets and rebuild confidence among investors. In 2003, American Funds received $65 billion in cash inflows, a new record for the mutual fund industry. One analyst compared this achievement to winning the World Series and the Super Bowl in the same year.

The seeds for Jason and Tom's partnership in the world of mental performance training were planted in October 2008, when the stock market lost more than 1,000 points—trading under 8,000 for the first time in years. Many people in the financial markets—and financial advisors, in particular—were extremely nervous. On the day of the 1,200-point market drop, Tom got a number of calls from advisors—most of them in the top 5 percent of their firms in revenue. Even with that success and experience, they had some panic in their voices. They asked him over and over, "What do we do now?"

Before getting into business coaching, Tom was very successful in another kind of coaching—on the basketball floor. At age twenty-five, he took over a team that had twenty-one consecutive losing seasons. In his second year as coach, the team went 20–5. The speech Tom gave those investment advisors came directly from the lessons he had learned during those first two seasons coaching the college team—that it is crucial to learn how to execute during times of adversity.

A few months later, Tom was reading an article in *Men's Health* about Jason's first book, *10-Minute Toughness*. The book was born from Jason's research and clinical experience with world-class athletes. It unlocked the "why" of elite mental performance—the science behind the success patterns that high achievers use. Tom bought it and read it several times, studying the principles in detail. Jason's research and real-world experience with elite athletes almost perfectly dovetailed with Tom's work as a high-level business coach. The message in the book—on simple steps to increasing your mental performance in business and life—spoke directly to the challenges Tom's advisor clients were facing. It was as if they had been working together for twenty years.

The stock market continued to struggle through 2009, and Tom flew around the country giving speeches and seminars for investment advisors, helping them learn how to guide their clients through a historically rough time. He began recommending Jason's book during his speeches, promoting it as the premier mental playbook for handling adversity. Jason and Tom got together in 2011, and in their first few conversations, they came to realize two fascinating things about the world of high achievement.

First, the greatest athletes and the greatest businesspeople are incredibly similar in their wiring. They think in many of the same ways, and they're built with the same kind of competitiveness. While Jason and Tom were using different terminology, they found they were really speaking the same language. The best coaches in both sports and business are expert "practical psychologists." They're perceptive evaluators, and they know how to figure out what makes a person tick. They understand the best approaches to take to reach different kinds of people.

Second, Jason and Tom saw that many, many people in both the sports and business arenas were being held back because they believed in a common misconception. The greatest athletes and businesspeople *are* different from average achievers—and some of the differences are innate. Some people are just faster, taller, stronger, or smarter than the rest of us. But *most* of the difference between the highest achievers and the average achievers is in how they think and how they prepare.

You can learn it, and you can grow it. That's the message Jason and Tom have shared in a series of training seminars around the country since late 2011. At their Organize Tomorrow Today workshops, they have been giving executives and salespeople a set of real-world techniques developed from the worlds of peak mental performance in sports and business to think better, prepare better, and achieve more.

That isn't just marketing copy.

Jason and Tom have coached not only professional athletes and financial advisors, but also executives of both large and small corporations, attorneys, physicians, insurance professionals, and others. No matter the industry, clients testify that the Organize Tomorrow Today program does two important things: it significantly reduces stress, and it creates more success.

That success isn't abstract or hard to define. It's measured in real-world financial results every quarter and every year. As word started to get out about the results Jason and Tom were helping people achieve, many different kinds of organizations tried to figure out how they were able to coach those teams to those kinds of gains. They couldn't, so they hired Jason and Tom, who have now used the principles behind Organize Tomorrow Today to train thousands more executives, managers, and salespeople.

Charlie Munger is well known for opening the minds of people in businesses of all shapes and sizes. One of Munger's most famous concepts is one he calls the "Lollapalooza Effect"—which is what occurs when strong forces work together to produce an exponential result much more substantial than what each force could produce individually.[2]

Jason and Tom believe that's what they've found with their Organize Tomorrow Today program—a way to exponentially improve the way you function in business and in life.

As a team, they've distilled their more than forty years of experience coaching athletes, executives, and salespeople at the very top of their disciplines. They've seen what works and what doesn't. Their Organize Tomorrow Today program condenses those success patterns into a streamlined set of core habit-building principles anyone can use. They are the same principles that their athletic clients have used to win World Series titles and Olympic gold medals, and that their professional clients have used to shatter revenue and sales records and create millions of dollars in new business.

The strategies are real, and you can incorporate them into your routine right away.

HOW?

One of Tom's mentors during his basketball coaching career (and on into his next life as a business coach) was the legendary UCLA coach John Wooden—who won ten national titles in a twelve-year stretch, in part by emphasizing the fundamentals of the game.

At the beginning of every season, Coach Wooden would begin the team's first practice the same way. No matter how much experience his players had, he started with the basics. He explained very specifically how to put on socks in a way that would prevent blisters, and how to get the laces on each shoe to sit flat to provide the most security and support.

As all great coaches know, skill mastery depends on learning through repetition, one step at a time. In basketball, you must learn to hold the ball correctly before you can even consider shooting it. The approach in *Organize Tomorrow Today* follows the same building-block principles; it shows you how to identify the fundamentals, then slowly (and certainly) move to mastery.

This book is made up of eight simple, concrete, easy-to-understand concepts:

- Organize Tomorrow Today
- Choose Wisely
- Maximize Your Time
- Win Your Fight-Thrus
- Evaluate Correctly
- Learn How to Talk to Yourself
- Learn How to Talk with Others
- Become Abnormal

They work together as a performance improvement plan for both work and life—but you don't even have to master them all to get a benefit. In fact, Jason and Tom don't want you to tackle them all.

Channel capacity is the key. One of the biggest mistakes people make in business and in life is that that they try to change too many things too quickly. You see it on New Year's Day, when so many people resolve to change everything they eat and go to the gym five times a week. After a burst of early enthusiasm for the new goal, reality sets in, and it gets harder and harder to cope with all the wrenching changes. At that point, it only takes a few days of "failure" to get discouraged and pitch the whole plan.

Instead, as you read the book, think about which of the eight concepts address some of the issues you're having in your professional or personal life. Pick the *one* that resonates the most. Start with that, and commit to following the step-by-step guidelines in that chapter. The key to high-level success is to pick one thing to change—yes, just one—and master it. The title of this book, *Organize Tomorrow Today*, comes from the concept that has been the most popular starting point among the attendees at Jason and Tom's seminars (which is also why it's the first one we cover).

If all you take from this book is a single, concrete change from one of the eight concepts, it's enough for you to make a true breakthrough to the next level of success—however you define it.

Jason and Tom are realists. The "law" of human channel capacity pretty much dictates that, at most, you're going to be able to successfully incorporate three of these ideas. So think of the material below as a sort of menu of improvement strategies. We'll show you eight dishes. All of them have been prepared by master chefs, and all of them will give you the nutrition you need. Sample them all, begin by choosing the three that resonate the most with you and then from there choose your favorite to be the main entrée, then attack. Over time, you can build on them, one concept at a time.

The rules are simple and straightforward, but this isn't some kind of "get-rich-quick" plan. You'll have to put in the work and change some habits to see improvement. It isn't any different from building your body in the gym, or improving a sports skill through practice. Follow steps in the chapters and hold yourself accountable for the results, and we guarantee that you can find the kind of performance gains that athletes, executives, and salespeople spend tens of thousands of dollars to achieve.

In *Organize Tomorrow Today*, you're getting your success pattern blueprint—a complete plan that builds on the little victories and establishes the long-term productive habits that will let you take control of your time and your life. That said, at the beginning and end of every seminar Jason and Tom teach, they offer one simple "warning" to the class, and they'll share it here, too: They are firm believers in increasing knowledge through training and through learning "best practices." But knowing something doesn't change your life. *Doing* something does. Getting through this book (or a class) is one thing, but there's a huge difference between acquiring information and *understanding* it. And there's an even wider gap between understanding it and implementing it, or actually *doing* it. This is why there is such an emphasis in *Organize Tomorrow Today* to avoid trying to master all eight concepts at once. Doing so is a recipe for inaction and failure. Success comes in one dedicated and focused step at a time.

The most successful people we see are the ones who take this information and use it in real life. Every day.

Follow the template, and you're getting a playbook for speeding up the process of getting from information acquisition to skill implementation.

Jason and Tom call it the Owner's Manual for Doers.

Let's get started.

1

ORGANIZE
TOMORROW TODAY

College football is one of the most competitive arenas around—in sports or business. The competition doesn't just happen on the field, during the season. Recruiting is a brutal business, and training eighteen-year-olds to succeed on both the field and in the classroom is a complicated job.

That's why what Nick Saban has done since 2000, first at LSU and now at Alabama, is so amazing. Saban's teams have won four national championships in that span. Only Bear Bryant, Alabama's coach from 1958 to 1982, won more.

It's tempting to attribute Saban's success to great recruiting and superior in-game coaching tactics. But in reality, most of the other power programs handle those parts of the process in a very similar way. And Saban's offensive and defensive schemes have always been considered pretty straightforward.

What Saban does differently—and what causes his program to be the one that other top schools try to copy—is redefine "success" for each individual player and coach working under him. Coaches and players at Alabama don't talk about winning and losing. They talk about consistency of preparation and effort, and about consistently excelling at the few core priority tasks they have each day.

Coach Saban doesn't ask his players and coaches to accomplish everything in a given day, and he doesn't require them to do everything they possibly can to "improve." He knows that if players are trying to focus on "everything," in essence they are focused on nothing. He teaches the fundamentals, and he helps them establish their priorities for the next day—and the next week, and the next season. These priorities become known as "the process."

In sports or business, the art of improvement comes from the skill of establishing those few daily priorities and benchmarks the same way Coach Saban does. It comes from doing it ahead of time, so you can establish where your attention needs to fall—which gives your conscious and subconscious mind direction and calm.

In our world, we call this process "Organizing Tomorrow Today."

You've probably jotted out a to-do list on a Post-It note and stuck it to the side of your computer monitor. Or maybe you've even built an elaborate "to-do" system on your smartphone or calendar. We're not here to tell you that your method—if you have one—is worthless or wrong. The goal here is to puncture the myth that the highest-achieving people in sports and business are the ones who get the most done, and to get you to stop chasing that as your goal. Coach Saban would be the first one to say that isn't what works.

One of our favorite quotes comes from Stephen Covey, author of the international bestseller *The 7 Habits of Highly Effective People*. He said, "The noise of the urgent creates the illusion of importance." Even the best-intentioned people fall into that trap every day. They confront their own to-do list—either the one in their head or the one they've written down somewhere—and put out the fires causing the most smoke, or the ones that are easiest to pick off. There's no question it can be satisfying to check a particularly troublesome or annoying problem off the list once it's been handled—or to clean up two or three simple tasks—but that doesn't mean you've spent your time in the most effective way.[1]

In our experience, those who enjoy the most success are the ones who do the best job prioritizing the day's activities and accomplishing the most important tasks—not the greatest *number* of tasks. It's a skill even the most successful people can lose track of along the way.

> In our experience, those who enjoy the most success are the ones who do the best job prioritizing the day's activities and accomplishing the most important tasks—not the greatest *number* of tasks.

One of Tom's most successful clients was rated one of the top ten financial advisors in the country. He has hundreds of millions of dollars under advisement, and a long track record of accomplishing the important tasks in his business. But recently, he called Tom with an urgent request for help—and he wasn't somebody to call very often.

Here's how the conversation went:

Tom: What's going on?

Advisor: My business isn't where I want it to be. . . . Instead of me running it, it's running me. I need your help.

Tom: Okay. . . . Today is Thursday. How many days this week have you gone into your office with the names of clients you were going to speak to that day written down, along with a summary of what you wanted to talk about?

Advisor: That's it! I stopped getting organized for the next day. I forgot. . . . Thank you!

That prioritizing principle was the one adjustment Tom's client needed to get back to continuing his elite-level performance and feeling in control of his life again.

Another advisor had started her career strong, far exceeding her targets for each of her first three years. But then she hit a wall, and after two years of weak results was in danger of "flunking out" and leaving the business. At the suggestion of her regional leader, she attended class, where she learned to Organize Tomorrow Today.

Over the first few months after the class, she became addicted to organizing her business life. Within a year, she was one of the highest producers in her region, and a few years after that she was given leadership responsibilities with her region. Within five years, she had been promoted to the home office, where she had even more responsibility.

All after changing one thing.

THE PROCESS

Written lists are as old as, well, writing, but there's solid scientific evidence that they work better than keeping a list in your head— or even tapping one out on a keyboard. Researchers Pam Mueller and Dan Oppenheimer from Princeton University and UCLA found that students who wrote out notes longhand retained more and had a better conceptual understanding of the material than students who typed notes on a keyboard.[2]

Why? The physical act of writing stimulates an area of the brain called the reticular activating system (RAS), which is responsible for filtering information into the "instant access" and "deep storage" folders in your mind. It tells your brain that the information is important and needs to be kept to the forefront. It also primes your subconscious mind to get to work—which is why you hear so many stories of songwriters and comedians keeping a notepad by the bed to record lyrics or jokes that leap out in the middle of the night.[3]

Still, to get the full benefit of that fun physiological fact, you have to approach your list-making with some sophistication. You can take your pen and paper and start creating a laundry list of tasks that need to be finished, but unless you learn to impose some important filters on those tasks, you'll struggle to improve your efficiency.

Ask yourself if this sounds like you. You make out a to-do list with eight or ten items on it, and you start your day with some of the easier items on the list because you want to build some momentum. You'll handle the more complicated or problematic things a little later—once you've had some coffee, or maybe just after lunch. Or maybe at 3:00, when you have a clear window of time to really focus.

It's a natural tendency. The only problem is, it doesn't work. What ends up happening is that you put in a full day, checking off item after item, but you get to the end of the day without tackling the most important items. That produces stress and tension for the next day, and the feeling that you're falling behind—even though you're as busy as can be.

As we alluded to before, the key point is to understand that high achievers aren't necessarily completing more tasks. They're accomplishing more of the ones *that matter most.* As busy as people are these days, it is no longer possible to get it all done. The key to success has become prioritization. Prioritization may very well be the most underrated skill of the highly successful. It is what will make the single biggest difference between being busy and being productive. Highly successful people never get it all done in any one given day—but they always get the most important things done each day.

> Highly successful people never get it all
> done in any one given day—but they always get
> the most important things done each day.

It doesn't matter how organized, efficient, and energized you are. You will *never* get everything done every single day. That's just too high a bar to set. But you can resolve to *always* get to your most important tasks and conversations.

The Organizing Tomorrow Today strategy will help you do this. It starts with getting into the habit of taking about five minutes the day before to identify your priorities for the upcoming day. But instead of creating that laundry list we talked about before, you produce a simple, curated, prioritized list.

The first part of the list is called the "3 Most Important." It's just as it sounds—the three most important tasks you need to complete the next day. Your goal is to build out your list of three tasks, along with the time of day you'll have each one completed.

It's important to say that the tasks on this list aren't full-blown projects that must have all of their steps completed in a single day. The tasks can and should be specific component tasks that work as a part of the whole. The key is to list important, ambitious, but realistic tasks that can reasonably be completed during the day. Small, day-to-day successes are the building blocks of achievement.

The second part of the list is called the "1 Must." Once you've determined your "3 Most Important," you choose the "1 Must" from these three items. It is the single most important task or conversation you need to have that day. Multiple studies in the subfield of quantitative behavioral analysis pioneered by B. F. Skinner in the 1930s have proven what you probably already intuitively feel day-to-day—that if you start moving on a task or a project, it's easier to keep in motion on that task. It's the human brain's version of the classic physics rule of inertia: A body in motion tends to stay in motion, while a body at rest tends to stay at rest. The best way to promote action is to identify just one thing, and then attack. Picking that most important to-do item creates the momentum.[4]

> **A body in motion tends to stay in motion,
> while a body at rest tends to stay at rest.**

Unfortunately, many people build a massive list of daily expectations and insist to themselves that they will always get the most important things done. But channel capacity is quickly reached, and you get overwhelmed. Then it gets easier and easier to just cast the list aside with some vague idea that you'll try again the next day—or lie to yourself and say that, since you accomplished eight or nine "little things," you had a productive day, even though you didn't finish anything of true importance.

To set yourself on the right track, ask yourself those two critical questions: (1) What are the three most important things I need to get done tomorrow? and (2) What is the single most important task I *must* get done? The questions work within your brain's "channel capacity" to give you direction and prioritization in manageable doses. When you start your day, you know the three most important things you need to get done by the end of the day, and you know which of those three things is the big, glow-in-the-dark priority. You'll be amazed at how much clearer your decision-making becomes—and how much more efficiently you'll use your time—just by taking this simple organizational step.

Once you've created your list, remember that it doesn't exist in a vacuum. You can have a big master list somewhere of all the things you want to get done this week, this month, or this year. The "3 Most Important / 1 Must" list is simply the priority filter that goes on top of the master list—the day-to-day action plan that puts things in motion.

To use another analogy from the sports world, a big-picture item on the to-do list for a given baseball season might be to win the division. But on day one, winning the division isn't a part of an individual player's "3 Most Important" list. The prioritized list for the day would be something like completing a full stretching routine, taking fifty quality cuts in the batting cage, and playing fifteen minutes of long-toss.

One caveat: With all of this introspection and personal list making, it can be easy to give the human communication part of the "3 Most Important / 1 Must" less attention than it deserves. It's a common mistake—both for people who don't have a lot of day-to-day interaction with people outside the office, and those whose businesses rely on things like sales calls or prospect meetings. In either case, it's tempting to close your door and burrow into your work, communicating mostly by email or text message. But we believe—and strongly recommend—that you reemphasize the personal element of your "3 Most Important / 1 Must" and make those connections directly, either face to face or over the phone. There's often a direct correlation between in-person communication and your level of success.

PREPARED MEANS CONFIDENT

It's fair to say that all of us face some level of adversity each and every day. Our clients have recognized that being organized and prepared for adversity significantly increases confidence. To give you an idea of how this works in practice, we'll use two of our recent clients as an example.

Tina moved out to California with the dream of becoming an actress. She spent years working on her craft and taking side jobs to pay the bills while she waited for that big break. With her talent, natural good looks, and relentless work ethic, she scored a few smaller roles in shows you've heard of, but she wasn't able to find consistent work that would let her put down permanent roots.

One summer, a family friend who knew about Tina's situation came to her with a job proposition. He owned a health-care company, and he was always on the lookout for charismatic people to work in sales roles. Tina had never given sales much thought—unless waiting tables counts as sales—but her bank account told her she should think seriously about the offer. She came to us to get some sense of how to organize herself and develop the skills she needed to be successful in a sales role. Tina is a naturally confident person, and she felt like she would be a good salesperson—as long as she was able to come into each of the meetings prepared.

We started her with Organize Tomorrow Today (OTT) as one of her first tools. She committed to spending a few minutes at the end of every day writing down the three most important tasks she would undertake the next day. By clearly delineating her priorities and breaking the tasks down into manageable—and accountable—chunks, Tina was able to take in a massive amount of new information and build a variety of new skills without feeling overwhelmed. She never got to the end of the day worried that she was unprepared for what was coming next.

One of Tina's daily lists looked something like this. Notice where Tina has placed the most important items in her day—at the very beginning:

3 MOST IMPORTANT	
Task	**To Be Completed**
Proactive Sales Contacts (Sylvain, James, and Tracy)	8:30 a.m.
Complete product line summary for client TS	9:15 a.m.
Talk to Matt B, sales mentoring advice	10 a.m.
1 Must	
Proactive Sales Contacts (Sylvain, James, and Tracy)	

One of our Major League Baseball clients used the "3 Most Important / 1 Must" technique in the period leading up to becoming a free agent, because his goal was to sign a lucrative multiyear contract that would take him to the end of his career. He knew that the right deal would set his family up financially and carry him through the ten years of Major League service that would guarantee his full pension. He also knew that unless he dedicated all of his energy to improving his performance, it would be tough to find a team that would make a good match.

Michael came to us to get some sense of how to organize himself and sharpen the skills he needed to be successful. He's a naturally confident person, and he felt like his best pitching was still ahead of him—as long as he was able to come into each day prepared with a game plan for success.

With the OTT tool, Michael committed to spending a few minutes at the end of every day reviewing the three most important tasks he would undertake the next day, and the single most important task he had to complete. His "3 Most Important" looked like this:

3 MOST IMPORTANT	
Task	**To be Completed**
Follow 100 percent of strength and conditioning workout	9:00 a.m.
Complete mental workout before each game/workout	10:00 a.m.
Deep practice—Slider (15 minutes, all non-game throwing days)	11:00 a.m.

Michael's "1 Must" rotated between the tasks shown above, having conversations with his pitching coach about mechanics, and conferring with the starting catcher on scouting reports of the teams he'd be pitching against. He also reached out to several prominent retired pitchers he knew to get some insight into how they strategized against different kinds of batters. On other days, he talked to team strength coaches and nutritionists to get his body in peak condition.

As a result, Michael was clear on the process he needed to follow to be totally prepared for game day. Having a game plan gave him renewed purpose and passion for the daily work. He felt confident because he had a plan that he knew would work. His increased confidence allowed him to not get caught up in results and to stay calm during the heat of competition.

Michael was able to make a massive amount of measurable improvement while keeping his confidence high. He felt comfortable every day knowing what he needed to do to *control* his success.

Identifying daily priorities might seem like an obvious or insignificant step to take, but writing your most important tasks down the previous night turns your subconscious mind loose while you sleep and frees you from worrying about being unprepared. You'll probably find that you wake up with great ideas related to the tasks or conversations that you hadn't even considered!

It's important to pay attention to the mechanics of making the lists, because the goal is always to set up a daily habit with as few roadblocks to implementation as possible. If something is pure torture for you to do, you're probably not going to be able to keep it up over time. And this tool is one you need working for you every day from now own.

DON'T WAIT UNTIL
THE END OF THE DAY

To start, don't wait until the very end of the day to make your list. We've used this tool with thousands of clients and conference attendees, and the overwhelming feedback we get is that the closer you get to the end of the day—whether that's the time you leave your office or before you switch over to family mode at home— the less likely you are to set aside the time to actually do it.

It's worth repeating: don't wait until it's the very last thing in your day to organize for tomorrow. Do it a bit earlier in your day to give yourself a fighting chance to complete it. It's that important.

> It's worth repeating: don't wait until it's the very last thing in your day to organize for tomorrow. Do it a bit earlier in your day to give yourself a fighting chance to complete it. It's that important.

We've found that the window between lunchtime and 3 p.m. seems to be the sweet spot for making the OTT plan. In fact, many of our clients make it a rule not to take the first bite of their lunch until they've built out their OTT plan for the next day.

The next big mistake to avoid is drilling too deeply. This tool is designed for you to pick the big, important priorities for the next day. Writing your list should take you about five minutes. If you're having trouble, keep in mind that the goal isn't to make an exhaustive list of everything you need to do tomorrow. You're developing the ability—and the habit—of prioritizing. If you don't do it for yourself, other people will do it for you—or, more accurately, *to* you.

It will be difficult at first, but you need to train yourself to understand that checking off everything on your big to-do list isn't the goal. Highly successful people get the most important things done every day—"3 Most Important," and "1 Must"—and do their best to get everything else done in the time that's left. On most days, you're going to have things pop up that will require your attention at some point. How many times have you closed yourself into your office to really bear down on an important project, only to remember something urgent—but not really important—that you need to take care of?

For example, you forgot to schedule that doctor's appointment your daughter needs before the beginning of the school year. You tell yourself it will only take a minute, and you go online to look up the doctor's phone number. You make the call, but you're placed on hold, so you surf the web for a bit. You finally make the appointment, but in the meantime, you've found an interesting article and finish it up. You look up and it's forty minutes later—and you've solved the appointment problem, but haven't even started any of the day's most important tasks.

Use your smartphone to create a holding area for those urgent-but-not-overly-important tasks, and resolve to work your way down that list only after you've completed the items from your OTT list. If you get to the point where you don't think you'll be able to address something from that separate holding-area list, you have the chance to decide if something from that list needs to make it onto the "3 Most Important" for the next day.

What you're doing is imposing intention onto what you do. Instead of operating day-to-day in reaction to events, you're setting priorities and getting out in front of things. You're training yourself to get better at prioritizing. And when you are better at prioritizing, you will be surprised how quickly you get things accomplished: we've found that, generally speaking, it takes somewhere between two and three hours of focused attention for a person to complete all three of their most important tasks for a given day.

Does this mean that you'll never have an emergency or need to put out a fire? Of course not. Life happens. But the most successful people have figured out a simple, effective technique for winning: they plan on emergencies happening every day.

That's right. The most successful people know that just about every day, surprises will happen, and plans will change. They plan on it, and they aren't surprised by it.

Emergencies typically don't start happening until mid to late morning, and that is precisely why successful people get their "3 Most Important / 1 Must" tasks completed early in the day. The majority of our clients have learned the value of completing the most important activities before 9:30 or 10:00 a.m.

It may not be possible to get all three of your most important tasks done that early each day. If a task involves another person, that person may not be an early bird. But we highly suggest that you take advantage of the "get it done early" principle whenever humanly possible.

Surprises are much, much easier to deal with when you have an effective handle on the most important things on your plate. Prioritizing and starting early will give you the energy to fight off a common temptation—to push one of the items on the list off to the next day. And you will be tempted: inevitably, you'll be right in the middle of something when you realize that you're up against the time by which you said you'd complete one of your important tasks or conversations. Instead of telling yourself, "I'll do it later"—which is code for "I'm not going to do it"—refuse to forfeit that score for the day.

Don't take a zero.

If nothing else, commit to spending one minute on the important task. It will help reinforce the prioritization skills you're developing. Taking a zero on one of your most important tasks is the equivalent of a professional athlete losing a game by forfeit. Passing altogether on your priorities completely erodes mental toughness. Commit to giving at least one minute of attention to each of your priorities, and you will find yourself, sooner rather than later, developing the mental toughness needed for winning consistently.

> Taking a zero on one of your most important tasks is the equivalent of a professional athlete losing a game by forfeit. Passing altogether on your priorities completely erodes mental toughness.

Having that kind of intentional, clear-headed approach to her day-to-day made all the difference for Tina. Within a year, she had become the most successful sales rep at her company. Last year, her bonus was bigger than she had made in any three years as an actress. When she tells the story, she laughs and says she should quit and go back to Hollywood to chase her dream now that she has so much freedom and control.

Michael not only got the big contract, but he's still pitching to a high level in the major leagues to this day. He's tuned his body and mind so well that he isn't remotely considering retiring. He's having too much success—and too much fun.

WHY IT WORKS: TURN YOUR
MIND LOOSE WHILE YOU SLEEP

We ask the folks who take our seminars (or read this book) to start with one rule when they begin the improvement process. In the seminars, the Organize Tomorrow Today rule is the one most people pick to do first. It's probably because the rule is so satisfying on a day-to-day basis, and because it has such a strong grounding in both science and common sense.

When you go to the effort to make a prioritized list of what you need to do the next day, you're essentially opening a loop in your mind. As you sleep, your brain will automatically start preparing for the successful closing of those loops. It's known as the "Zeigarnik Effect." In the 1920s, Russian psychology researcher Bluma Zeigarnik quantified the phenomenon after her professor, Kurt Lewin, noticed that waiters who hadn't been paid for an order had much more recall of the details of those orders than they did for orders that had been paid. Working from Zeigarnik's research, Lewin came up with the concept of "task-specific tension," which persists in both the conscious and subconscious mind until the task is completed.[5]

In other words, the mind doesn't like unfinished business! High-level mathematicians and successful writers have been using this technique for years as a tool for pushing their work forward. Before going to bed, they take a few minutes to read over the mathematical or literary work they did during the day—especially if they've reached a plateau or feel stuck. The mind then works all night to close the loop, and they wake up in the morning with "inspiration." It seems magical, but it isn't so much magical as it is the result of effective priming of the mental pump.

The OTT principle and prioritization with a list make sense. If you could eliminate—or at least significantly reduce—certain anxieties in your life with a simple, five-minute ritual, why wouldn't you try it?

USE MOMENTUM AS A CATALYST

If you can go into your next day feeling more prepared and less anxious, you will project that comfort and confidence in what you do. Instead of spinning your wheels early and trying to generate momentum, you'll come in with momentum already in place. And when you knock off that "1 Must" from the list, you'll be generating even more momentum—not fooling yourself with little pretend "victories" in the stuff that didn't really matter in the first place.

You really will be staying in motion.

Organizing Tomorrow Today hones your prioritizing skill—and prioritizing is what will make the single biggest difference between being productive and being busy. Busy people don't necessarily get much done. Productive people do.

"Busy" isn't what gets rewarded long-term in the marketplace. "Productive" is.

> "Busy" isn't what gets rewarded long-term in the marketplace. "Productive" is.

You'll certainly be challenged on a day-to-day basis by the "noise of the urgent," but having this tool in place will help you make the decisions that will separate you from the average.

The Big Why: The most successful people don't get everything done. They get the most important things done. By organizing and prioritizing your effort toward the core tasks you need to accomplish, you create momentum and confidence. You go into attack mode.

The Inversion Test: One of our favorite devices to use within each rule is to apply a lesson that Charlie Munger adapted from German mathematician Carl Jacobi: to better understand a principle, invert it. It's simply looking at the opposite side—in this case, what happens if you *don't* organize tomorrow today.[6]

If you don't organize, you begin the day on defense. You're extremely busy, but not very productive. If you want to slow your progress, don't organize tomorrow today.

Act Now: The mechanics of how you make your lists aren't as important as actually doing it. You can use a small notebook, a pad of paper, or an app on your smartphone.

Spend three to five minutes preparing your own "3 Most Important" tasks or conversations for tomorrow, and the "1 Must"—or main priority—out of the three. Remember, the goal is to schedule completion of these tasks as early as possible in your day.

Some examples from our clients:

PRO ATHLETE	
1. Complete my Mental Workout before the game	11:30 a.m.
2. Complete 30 minutes film study on opponent	1:15 p.m.
3. Do 100 percent rehab after the game	10:15 p.m.
FINANCIAL ADVISOR	
1. Contact two "elephants" (current high-net-worth clients)	8:45 a.m.
2. Contact one prospect	9:15 a.m.
3. Ask one time for a referral or first face-to-face meeting	11:00 a.m.
PHYSICIAN	
1. Perform 30 minutes of cardio exercise (heart rate 130+ for 30 minutes)	6:00 a.m.
2. 60 minutes case prep	7:00 a.m.
3. Contact one COI (center of influence)	9:15 a.m.

2

CHOOSE WISELY

Albert Einstein came up with a popular (and fascinating) list of what he called the five levels of intelligence:

1. Smart
2. Intelligent
3. Brilliant
4. Genius
5. Simple

The step beyond genius? To be able to see beyond the chaos and complications of everyday life and identify the most important solutions to the most important problems.

Simplicity.[1]

You don't have to have superhuman intellectual powers to take away a powerful message from Einstein's theory. The key is learning how to choose wisely.

We've talked about the scientific definition of "channel capacity," and how it relates to the human mind. But a scientist determining how many numbers a person can remember is very different from crawling on your belly in the mud for miles, pushing yourself to the physical and mental breaking point and beyond. Let us tell you about Bobby Gassoff.

Bobby grew up the son of defenseman Bob Gassoff of the National Hockey League's St. Louis Blues. Bob was tragically killed in a motorcycle accident before Bobby was born. Bobby was a hockey natural, just like his dad, and went to the University of Michigan on a hockey scholarship. In 1994, he was an important member of the team that won the NCAA championship.

After college, Bobby started on the traditional hockey prospect road, playing in the minor leagues with the hope of working his way up to the NHL. But not long into that process, he hung up his skates and set his sights on something much more important than hockey. He started an intense training regimen with the goal of joining the Navy SEALs—one of the most elite fighting units in the world. When Bobby got to BUDS—basic underwater demolition training—he was in peak physical and mental condition. So was everybody else in his class. They were the "best of the best" from the armed forces.

But during "hell week," these trainees would run the equivalent of three full marathons while carrying hundreds of pounds of gear. They would crawl through the mud and sand, get dropped miles out to sea, and have to swim back—or drown. And they would do it all soaking wet, freezing cold, and on less than thirty minutes of sleep per night. This regimen would separate the toughest from the rest.

By the third day of hell week, the skin around Bobby's armpits and groin had been worn away by wet sand. He was completely exhausted, and he still had four days to go. That night, one of his teammates—a Navy pentathlete and the best runner and swimmer in the group—rang the bell and quit.

Despite the nearly overwhelming urge to follow his teammate over to the bell and ring out, Bobby decided he would narrow his mind to a single focus point. He would concentrate on just one thing—the very next step—because the thought of what was coming the next day and the day after that was just too overwhelming to consider.

When the trainees finally got a few minutes to wolf down some food in between activities, the instructors would walk among the exhausted men and call out the laundry list of brutal things that were scheduled for the rest of the day—a tactic designed to root out trainees who could be distracted or disheartened.

A six-mile run.

Two hours of surf training.

Three hours on the obstacle course.

An eight-mile boat haul.

Bobby kept his "one step" focus, survived hell week, and graduated from SEAL training. Of the 240 men to start training, he was one of 24 to make it, and he was one of only 2 to graduate as an officer. He was—and is—one of the toughest people on the planet, and to this day, he still operates by the principles that got him through.

If that's the case for somebody like Bobby, what does it mean for the rest of us? As we touched on in the previous chapter, one of the most common traps to fall into in business and life is to try to focus on too much and lose focus on the really important things. People have a tendency to overcommit to others and to themselves. Doing so not only causes underperformance but also has a tremendously negative impact on confidence. When you commit to doing too much, you inevitably let other people down and unfortunately begin to send a message that you cannot be trusted.

It usually starts as something quite harmless but unfortunately snowballs quickly. It could be something as simple as telling a colleague you will help out with a task or even telling a loved one you will be home by a certain time. The next thing you know, you have become overwhelmed by your own mountain of responsibilities and you haven't left time for that colleague or loved one. You never intended to let someone else down but it just got away from you.

The problem is that this becomes habitual to the point where you know even when you are committing to certain things that there is a high likelihood you won't follow through when the time comes. This is a prime example of not choosing wisely. If you are trying to beat channel capacity, you will always lose. When you overload the system with requirements, the same thing happens to your mind that happens with an outdated computer running heavy-duty software. You start to freeze, and decisions get harder to make.

As we keep saying, you can't beat channel capacity.

In this chapter, we'll talk about learning how to choose wisely and pick that *one step* that is the next most important one in the progression. You'll learn how to attack that one step with your full attention, and then move on to the next—instead of overcommitting your way into mediocrity.

Doing it all—or being great at it all—should never be the goal.

Think about what the average office environment looks like. You're sitting at your desk, working on a document that has to get out the door by the end of the week. You hear your email chime, and you see the notification at the top of the screen, telling you that the message is from one of your colleagues. You click away from the document and scan the email, then type a quick response. Then you click back to where you left off on the document, and pick up your work again.

That might sound normal, or harmless, but every time you turn into one of those attention cul-de-sacs, you're making your mind work really hard to get up to speed on the new task, then making it work some more as you click back to where you were on the previous one. And that's a problem—remember channel capacity—because it's going to compromise your ability to do your best on the really important tasks.

Is it the end of the world if it happens once? Of course not. But does it ever happen just once? The reality is that we're always answering phones, looking at text messages, sending emails, or dividing our attention by surfing the web while we talk on the phone to a client. We're surrounded by distractions. The fact that multitasking is difficult for our brains doesn't mean you won't be able to juggle the balls and accomplish those other tasks. It just means that, if you constantly divide your attention, trying to do more than one thing at the same time, you're going to use a lot more energy and time to get things done than you need to. You're going to compromise your attention and miss some of the finer details.

You don't have to look very far to find examples to illustrate the same point at the organizational level. We see it all the time. A company will call a big meeting—often off-site—to get everybody together so the top execs can reveal what the new corporate strategy is. Then, the group gets presented with a laundry list of goals for the coming quarter or financial year. There are eight or twelve "metrics" and "measures," and it isn't usually clear which ones are most important. Because it's "important" and everybody is already together, the meeting is almost always scheduled for all or most of the day. But the reality is that everybody in the room has reached channel capacity by the first break.

Worse yet, even if the people in the audience understand the metrics and measurements and know which ones apply to them personally, they usually don't know how to prioritize them. They don't know which ones are the most important for them personally.

It happens the same way in the sports world. "Winning" is the same kind of top-level goal as "profit," but all of the additional responsibilities can get an athlete spinning his or her wheels. Imagine what happens to a college quarterback who gets picked in the first round of the NFL draft. He signs a large contract, and the team is expecting him to come in and (eventually) become the face of the franchise.

When minicamps start in the summer before his first season, the quarterback has a huge amount of work to do. He has to learn the playbook and integrate himself into the team. He has to show not only that he's willing to work hard and learn, but also that he can become a leader. In addition, the team expects him to make numerous public appearances and make himself available to the media. Not to mention the increase in expectations and demands from family and friends. It's really three or four different jobs in one. And we're talking about a player who is twenty-one or twenty-two years old, who has just been handed more money than most people will make in their entire career.

There's a lot to focus on, and there are a lot of ways to go off the tracks. Is it really a surprise that the players who narrowed their focus to a few critical goals and tasks—and basically operated as sports hermits for their first few seasons—are the ones who have had the most success?

Leading up to the 1998 NFL draft, Tennessee quarterback Peyton Manning was considered to be one of the top prospects in all of college football. Manning was considered to be intelligent and hard working, but his arm strength wasn't considered to be the strongest in the draft. Even though the Colts' scouts favored another quarterback, Colts general manager Ed Polian decided to pick Manning. Manning hit the ground running after the draft, focusing on one thing: burying himself at the Colts' team facility to learn the playbook. He was the Colts' starter from the first game of his rookie season, and he would go on to become one of the greatest quarterbacks of all time.

You are more like Peyton Manning than you think. He is not the most gifted athlete on the field, and other quarterbacks are stronger and faster and younger. Yet he is a consistent winner.

He walks up to the line of scrimmage with the play that has been called from the sidelines. Once the ball is snapped, he's going to have things coming at him from all angles. Throughout the day some things will go his way and some things won't. There may even be a time or two when he gets slammed to the turf and has to pick himself back up and go at it again.

You walk into your office and, chances are, things start immediately flying at you from all directions. Throughout your day, you'll feel ahead sometimes and behind other times. There may even be a time or two when you feel like a 350-pound lineman has just planted you into the dirt. Just like Manning, you have to find the strength to get back to your feet and re-engage.

Peyton Manning has been able to do it year after year after year because he chooses wisely and does one thing exceptionally well. He is relentless with his preparation—and you can be, too.

Choosing wisely is difficult because it is counterintuitive. It is much easier to put a laundry list together of all the possible things you need to get done each day than it is to actually choose your one most important task and then master it.

> Choosing wisely is difficult because it is counterintuitive. It is easier to put a list together of all the possible things you need to get done than it is to actually choose your one most important task and then master it.

INFORMATION ADDICTION

Think about that big off-site meeting we were just talking about a few paragraphs ago. At many of those meetings, organizations schedule training seminars to get big groups of employees "up to speed" on new techniques and strategies. If you've worked in corporate America for any amount of time, you're very familiar with the kind of training session we're talking about.

Now, you'll never hear us say that innovation is a bad thing, or that training employees for the skills you want to reward is a wasted effort. But think about the way the vast majority of those corporate training sessions work. You're handed a binder when you walk in (or directed to a URL to enter on your tablet). There's somebody standing in the front of the room with a big screen, getting ready to motor through fifty PowerPoint slides.

The information could be great. But setting the group up to be force-fed for hours at a time quickly creates an overload situation. You reach channel capacity before you even get to the first break.

And when that break comes, what happens? Everybody surges from their seats to hit the snack table to eat, drink, stretch, and chitchat about how they can't believe there's three more hours of this to go.

The data is important. But it's just washing over people who are too overwhelmed by the amount of information to be able to absorb it. All of that wasted information isn't even the worst part of it. The dirty little secret that gets left out of the accounting? Saturating people with information actually paralyzes action. Think about it: when people are overwhelmed, they typically freeze. Self-doubt slows action.

> Saturating people with information actually paralyzes action. Think about it: when people are overwhelmed, they typically freeze. Self-doubt slows action.

If you are a leader in your organization and are spearheading these meetings, you're not just paying for the conference space, hotel rooms, and catering: you're slowing your staff from doing their jobs. It can be a gigantic waste of time and money if you aren't giving people something that they can, with confidence, use to make a positive, measurable change. By overloading people with information you are essentially causing them to overcommit. If you are working for an organization and attending the meetings, two of the crucial skills you probably aren't learning are how to prioritize the information being poured into you and how to understand the point of equilibrium when it becomes actionable.

Technology makes some things better, but when it comes to this subject, it often makes things worse. We have the physical ability to "receive" way more information in the literal sense—thousands of emails in a folder, tens of thousands of documents on hard drive—than in the old days. But the technology doesn't do much to prioritize that information or steer it where it needs to go. It's like having an enormous fire hose at your disposal—one twenty times bigger than the normal size. But the hose shoots out so much water that when you try to hold onto the end you get flopped around like a fish.

CHOOSE WISELY

This isn't some kind of anti-progress or anti-technology rant. Cutting-edge information is the lifeblood of business, and it is crucial to understand how to digest it.

We run dozens of corporate training seminars every year for a variety of different organizations. We go into every one of them with a customized game plan, but the overall goal is always the same. Step by step, we intersperse very controlled amounts of information relevant to the business with direct, hands-on practice in implementing that information.

Even though we want to teach everything we know, we work very hard to respect channel capacity. We'll have discussions late into the evening about whether or not we should include that latest piece of information. In the end we usually finish the conversation with one of us saying, "When in doubt . . . delete." It's a lesson Jason learned from one of the greatest coaches of all time.

Dan Gable's wrestling teams at the University of Iowa won 15 NCAA team titles from 1976 to 1997. Individually, his wrestlers won 45 national titles and 106 conference championships during that time. Before becoming a coach, Gable had one of the most dominant careers in the history of wrestling, going 117–1 during his time at Iowa State, and winning the Olympic gold medal in Munich in 1972 without giving up a single point. He knows something about elite performance, and what you have to do to achieve it.

Years ago, Coach Gable told Jason that one of the basic fundamentals of his approach to competing—both as an athlete and as a coach—was "choosing wisely." To him, that meant not overcommitting. Gable learned the importance of identifying the right "critical factor" and directing his energy toward moving it.

In Dan Gable's world, not overcommitting allowed him to remain focused on what was most important, practicing every night until he was physically exhausted. It doesn't have to be so dramatic in your world, but it's important to understand the point.

At every seminar we teach, we introduce the attendees to the rules you're learning about in this book. Once we've covered what they are and how they're used, we ask everyone to choose just one thing they want to "nail"—to execute as completely as possible. Whether we're talking about NFL players or business professionals, the ones who set the records and make All Pro are the ones who choose wisely and relentlessly focus on improvement one step at a time.

Does this have the potential to sound simplistic, or even goofy? Sure.

THE POWER OF ONE

What Dan Gable instinctively knew at a young age—and what we try to establish in all of our work with athletes and businesspeople— is this: focusing on one primary task makes *action* much more realistic—one simple, positive change builds momentum and primes you for the next success.

> Focusing on one primary task makes *action* much more realistic—one simple, positive change builds momentum and primes you for the next success.

One of our clients, a very successful small-business owner named Todd, came in with an ambitious plan for the coming year. He was determined to push his business to the next level financially. He had made plenty of good decisions in the past to get to where he wanted to be, but he was looking for that one push he needed to move to the next level.

After hearing about the concepts you're learning here, Todd decided that the first step he was going to take was to commit to going through the one-hundred-second Mental Workout we teach in our seminars (which we will cover in Chapter 6). At precisely 5:30 every morning, he got up and found a quiet place to collect his thoughts—usually the kitchen table—before the hustle and bustle of his day started.

During the one minute and forty seconds it took him to do the Mental Workout, he went through a series of positive affirmations that reminded him of his strengths and goals. He visualized things he had done well the previous day and the steps he needed to take in the upcoming day to achieve his "win." It sounds like something out of an infomercial, but a year of focusing on one positive improvement later, Todd had lost fifty pounds and doubled his business.

It isn't magic. It is the natural byproduct of a phenomenon that social scientists have recognized for decades. Inertia is a powerful force in human behavior, but it only works when you use it in a focused way.

You need to choose, and choose wisely. Focusing on one thing promotes action. Learn to do less, but more often.

> Focusing on one thing promotes action.
> Learn to do less, but more often.

We've all been trained to believe that we can do vastly more at one time than we really can. This notion is instilled in us in many ways: by school, by the books we read, by what we watch on television, and even by the devices we carry around with us. We'll bet that many of you reading this book are "available" at least five more hours per day than you were ten years ago, simply because you have the ability to answer emails and text messages anytime—whether you're sitting at breakfast with your family or getting ready to shut things down for the night.

In many ways, that accessibility has built artificial, unattainable expectations. If information moves twenty-four hours a day, you have to be ready to act on it twenty-four hours a day—or at least that is how it seems. When expectations change—and you hold yourself to that relentless, multitasking standard—you're destined to fail, and you will likely be hard on yourself when you do.

That's the first step in the perfectionist cycle. It's a trap, and most people have found themselves stuck in it at some point. You try to do everything and be everything, then you fail at it and get discouraged. At some point, the discouragement makes you stop trying.

Another mistake—besides not focusing on the one primary goal you've chosen to pursue—can be choosing unrealistic goals. It's especially common when it comes to the goals that will take a while to achieve. One client came to one of our coaching sessions and told us his plan was to lose forty pounds and compete in a marathon within twelve months in addition to trying to grow his business by 30 percent. He went through all the steps the self-help books tell you to take—including telling friends about his goal so he would stay accountable and setting up a $1,000 charitable donation "penalty" if he didn't accomplish his goal. He changed his diet and cut 30 percent of his daily calories, and he started a punishing workout routine every morning at 5 a.m. and attempted to make multiple changes to how he ran his business.

We tried to redirect him to a more sustainable, long-term goal, but his mind was made up and he refused to believe in the power of channel capacity. Within six months, he had lost the weight and had signed up for the marathon. His business was showing signs of improvement but nothing was really showing up in his bottom line.

> We tried to redirect him to a more sustainable, long-term goal, but his mind was made up and he refused to believe in the power of channel capacity.

By the eighth month, the client had finished the marathon. He was so relieved not to have to follow the brutal diet and training routine he had established that he completely backed off working out. By the twelfth month he was two pounds heavier than he had been when he had started the whole process the year before and his production at work had remained flat throughout the entire year. Instead of choosing wisely, the client overcommitted. He worked harder than he ever had but really had nothing to show for it.

We don't tell that story to make you feel like it's pointless to set goals—or even to set ambitious goals. As you'll see throughout the book, the opposite is actually the case. We want you to set goals and be ambitious. But we want you to learn to set goals that are attainable and sustainable. We want you to choose wisely. One success should prime you for the next success, not become a point where you can bail out. We want you to build the habit of winning—not just have a onetime win.

In the early 1990s, Edward Jones was a much smaller operation than it is now, and it didn't have many million-dollar producers among its advisors. Tom developed an advanced training program for the company's highest-achieving young advisors that had as its centerpiece this concept of understanding a small group of principles and choosing one to attack. They learned to stay focused on that one goal, and they learned to choose the goal wisely.

Tom kept meticulous records of how the advisors who went through the program performed and compared them to a peer group of advisors who didn't get the training. For every dollar Edward Jones invested in training the experienced advisors, it got a return of $17 by the end of the first year—strictly by choosing wisely and respecting the "power of one."

SAYING NO

The biggest obstacle that will block you from improvement is committing to too much and getting overwhelmed.

It's an especially dangerous—and common—problem as you work your way higher and higher on the food chain of success. If you're a smart, ambitious person who wants to learn and get better, your own drive and determination can work against you.

In every class we teach, we'll see an energetic, smart, high-achieving student who goes along with what we're presenting, and at the end grabs one of us for a quick conversation. "I can't wait to get started," the conversation starts. "It's so clear and simple, and I think I picked it up pretty quickly. I'm going to start on three changes instead of one and jump-start the process."

It doesn't matter how smart or successful you are. Even if you can read two hundred pages a night and work twelve-hour days, you will bump up against the self-limiter of channel capacity. That's where saying no comes in.

And it's a talent many, many people either have never learned or have chosen to forget—usually out of desire to please others or to avoid having an "uncomfortable" conversation. If you're going to commit to doing one thing at a time, it means, by definition, that there are some things you aren't going to be doing.

Most people think of saying no as a "negative" thing, and that can certainly be true in some unpleasant cases. But for the most part, saying no to something just means you're saying yes to something else. All we want to teach you to do is make those decisions consciously—and not get pushed into them by the unintended consequences of a series of other decisions.

One extremely successful client of ours is a retired athlete who still lives in the town where he was a star player. He's a gregarious guy who loves to help, and as a result, he is constantly asked to give his time to various causes—everything from playing in charity golf tournaments to serving on volunteer boards and shooting public service commercials. For years, he was always game to help in any way he could—to the point where he was run ragged six days a week and more burned out than he'd ever been during his active days as a player.

He made one simple change: he placed a picture of his wife and kids on his desk next to the phone.

He didn't stop making commitments to help, but every time a call came in, he stopped for a moment and thought about what he was really saying yes—or no—to. Many times, he would tell the person on the line that he appreciated being asked, but that he had to decline. "If I say yes to you, I'm saying no to my wife and kids, and that's not the man I want to be," he said. "I hope you understand."

Unfortunately, most people confuse "urgent" with "important" and say yes to so many urgent things that they are in effect saying no to other things that are much more important.

> Unfortunately, most people confuse "urgent" with "important" and say yes to so many urgent things that they are in effect saying no to other things that are much more important.

Sometimes it takes some time for this lesson to sink in. When we come back to an area where we've recently run a seminar, we always get students who come back to attend another session. Inevitably, students will come back and take the class again, and they'll tell us that when they tried to incorporate three or even two of the rules at a time, they spun their wheels. When they went back to basics and committed to nailing just one, they saw results even they couldn't believe. They'd get more done by channeling that focus than they ever could multitasking on a variety of to-do tasks.

NAILING IT

What does "nailing it" mean?

If you've truly mastered one positive change, we call it "nailing it." It's become a popular shorthand catchphrase with many of our students. For you to have fully integrated the improvement and the changes it requires, it means that for three consecutive months, you've been able to complete the change on a daily basis 90 percent of the time or better.

Whatever improvement you choose—whether it's Organizing Tomorrow Today or committing to doing the Mental Workout—you need to be able to do it nine out of ten days for three months straight—with no excuses. If you can't do it, it means you need to increase your discipline or commit to a smaller level of intensity. Get started by proving to yourself that you can nail it, even if it's a smaller commitment. You can always increase later on. An essential element of performance is for people to learn to trust themselves. When you prove 90 percent of the time that you can nail it, you can't help but grow your confidence and self-trust.

Why does it work? Because simplicity, accuracy, and direction are a powerful combination. They provide the key to action that everybody needs—whether you're a financial advisor, an NFL wide receiver, or a road paver for the state highway department. At the core level, learning to "nail one thing" teaches you how to believe in yourself. Your confidence grows and your self-image aligns with the knowledge that you do what you commit to doing. You literally become a "winner."

The Big Why: The great myth of multitasking is that we're getting more accomplished by dividing our time and energy among all of the tasks clamoring for our attention. In reality, allowing your attention to be diverted from the step-by-step completion of your most important task triggers overload. And when you overload any system, it quits working and loses energy.

When you commit to not overcommitting and nailing just one task before you start the next, you're stacking the odds for success in your favor. Just remember to choose the most important task to attack first.

The Inversion Test: Put choosing wisely to the Charlie Munger inversion test and you get a simple output. What happens if you don't choose wisely, and you try to do too much? Overcommitting is counterproductive. Confidence erodes, failure becomes acceptable, and losing becomes a habit. The same thing happens when you try to carry too many groceries into the house from the car in an effort to "save time." You drop a bag and have a mess to clean up. Not only did you lose time, but you lost the eggs, too!

Act Now: Identify your "first step," in the form of one simple fundamental improvement you want to commit to for tomorrow. It doesn't have to be earth-shattering or complicated. Just something you can specifically identify and "nail."

Choose wisely.

Some examples from our clients:

PRO ATHLETE

No matter what, I am going to complete 30 minutes film study. My focus will be to more specifically identify one thing I can do to be more effective against the starting pitcher's most prominent pitch. This will be completed by 11:00 a.m. Getting it done early will give me a calm, confident, and aggressive mindset throughout the rest of my prep and into the game. What I will not do tomorrow is spend anytime playing video games.

FINANCIAL ADVISOR

The one thing I will attack tomorrow is making my proactive calls. I will make sure my first call of the day is to my most important client—NO EXCUSE. Everything after that will feel easy. I will not allow myself to spend more than 10 minutes reading headline financial news (I usually spend anywhere from 30 minutes to 60 minutes on this).

PHYSICIAN

I will process my most important overnight case report by 9:00 a.m. so the team has time to close it out before lunch. To do this, I will need to start on the case no later than 8:20.

3

MAXIMIZE YOUR TIME

Never mind not having enough time in the day. Randy Boll didn't have enough time in his year. Even after being named one of the top ten performers at his Fortune 500 company, he was gunning for more.

Randy told us he was hungry to reach his ultimate goal—to be No. 1 in his firm. He had always been a very organized and driven guy, and in the first few years in business, he had been able to crush his to-do list every day—which showed in his results. But recently, something had changed. The bar had been set higher, and he felt like there just weren't enough hours in the day to get it all done—and even if there were, he had so many more distractions these days.

Randy decided to start small and incorporate one of the basic ideas we're going to talk about in this chapter. He was going to do what we call "time maximization."

Over the course of the day, Randy—like anybody else—had a few minutes between meetings, or some time on the schedule he hadn't planned on because of a cancellation or an early finish. He resolved that whenever three minutes of time came free—and he found that this kind of pause occurred, on average, three times during the course of the day—he would ask himself a simple question. "What can I get done in the next three minutes?" And he'd consult the to-do list and knock out at least one important item from that list.

By maximizing time and attacking the "open space," instead of allowing himself to waste the time, Randy was essentially creating nine extra minutes per day, five days a week. That translates into forty additional hours per year. This one simple change gave Randy an extra week per year to gain an edge on the competition.

It wasn't a huge change, but it had huge results. Within a year, Randy broke the earnings milestone he had been dreaming about for all those years and was sitting in the top spot of his firm. He didn't do it with time *management*. He did it with time *maximization*.

––––––––

It might seem like a small distinction: management vs. maximization. But in terms of achievement, the difference is vast.

Traditional time management theories teach people how to do more with the time they have. Time maximization teaches you to create *more time*.

> Traditional time management theories teach people how to do more with the time they have. Time maximization teaches you to create *more time*.

The ultimate limitation for all of us is time. There's only so much time in the day, and you can only focus your attention on a certain number of things. Hundreds and hundreds of self-help books have focused on the concept of time management—ways to get your time organized and build your list of commitments into a manageable plan so you can be more "productive."

They mean well. But most successful people already manage their time. To break into the ranks of the highly successful, learning how to manage time better isn't going to change your life. Even if you come up with the perfect way to stack all of the pieces on your chessboard, you're limited by the size of the chessboard. And, more importantly, if you focus your attention on stacking those pieces and filling up the board, you're not necessarily creating a system that helps you put the right value on each of the pieces—or assign them the right amount of time.

Just because you have a lot of things to do and get them all done doesn't mean that all those things were done the right way, or that you're spending your time the way you want to be spending it.

Time *maximization* is very different. It is the search for both efficiency and productivity but also the act of prioritization at the same time. When you maximize your time, you're creating *more time* to do the important things. You're changing the size of the chessboard completely. It's working the other side of the ledger.

A simple analogy would be walking down into your basement and seeing water leaking from around one of the windows. You could manage that leak exceptionally well by coming up with a system of buckets to catch it, and purchasing drying equipment to keep the carpet from getting ruined, and then making a bunch of circuits downstairs to check to see if more water was coming in. Or, you could figure out how the water was getting in and fix the leak. Both skills are important, but one is *more* important.

In Chapter 1, we started the conversation about prioritizing your commitments for the next day through Organizing Tomorrow Today, or OTT. Really, that process is about assigning your time. You're predetermining what you will focus on the next day. If you're able to take that one simple step and be ready ahead of time, you've made a huge step toward successfully maximizing your time.

The next piece comes when you are actually executing on your organization. There, you're going to use three tools to maximize your time:

1. Attack the Open Space
2. Prioritize the Priorities
3. Trim the Fat

ATTACK THE OPEN SPACE

It starts with a simple question: What unit of time do you think in right now? In basic terms, the more successful you become, the smaller the unit of time you need to think in. Let us explain what that means.

> In basic terms, the more successful you become, the smaller the unit of time you need to think in.

When you're trying to manage your time, you look at a bunch of puzzle pieces and put them all together. That's fine, but it doesn't fully represent what happens in the real world. What really happens is that you have a collection of meetings, calls, emails, and other work to do during a given day, and most of the time those things don't happen in nice, clean intervals. You might have a call you need to be on that starts ten minutes early, or ends ten minutes late. An appointment may cancel, or some other responsibility didn't take as long as you thought it would.

What occurs when the "real world" happens and you have a soft spot of unscheduled time in between responsibilities? Most people exhale and spend a few minutes chatting with coworkers, surf the web, or make a call. Blowing off steam by stepping away from the work grind is fine, and it helps your long-term productivity.

But the success level you have—or the level you want to reach—should determine what unit of time you're thinking in.

Think about what happens when you reach a lull in your day. Let's say you have fifteen minutes before you have to go down the hall to a meeting. You might spend the time looking for deals on Amazon, absorb the latest celebrity gossip headlines at Gawker, or wander over to your friend's workspace to talk about last night's game. Maybe you have a puzzle game installed on your smartphone, so you tap away on that for a few minutes. Or, it might be time to check in with your mother, since it's been a few days.

TOP 7 TIME WASTERS
1. Personal email
2. Facebook
3. ESPN online
4. The Kardashians
5. Online News
6. Shopping sites
7. Google searches

Those are all "normal" ways to blow off some steam during the workday. They're probably so common that you almost don't even consciously think about doing them. But if you want to be one of the top producers in your firm, you need to do some things that are not "normal." You need to fill those gaps with something productive.

Take conscious control of those small gaps in your schedule by deciding what unit of time you're going to think in, and resolving that if you have a unit of time that size or larger, you're going to apply it to another one of the items on your to-do list.

In Jason's day-to-day practice, the two or three most important events of the day—usually client meetings—are time blocked, as are important phone calls, meetings, and travel. His "open space" unit of time is two minutes. Which means that if one minute of free time shows up in the schedule, he'll disengage and send a text message, check the baseball scores, or just close his eyes and re-charge. If two minutes or longer of open space show up in his day, he goes back to his expanded to-do list and asks himself what is one thing he can get done before he has to head on to his next commitment. If after completing his one thing there are still more than two minutes of unaccounted-for time available, he goes at it again, attacking his next one thing. And so on until the open space is smaller than his two-minute expectation or the open time is used up completely.

The more successful you become, the smaller that time incre-ment becomes. If you have a big staff or a lot of decisions on your plate, your window might be one minute. You can also create a wider increment, but you won't see much of the benefit of this tool if you expand the time segment out beyond fifteen minutes.

If you're a person who has never operated by a strict schedule (or you have trouble keeping the one you already have), I'm sure this seems like a severe or demanding way to operate. It's an un-derstandable reaction, and we won't tell you that the transition to a more structured approach will be completely painless. Once you've tried it, however, you will be impressed by what you can accomplish with a few minutes here and there. When identi-fying your "open space" unit of time, be sure to choose wisely. If you are new to this kind of strategy, it wouldn't make sense to set your number at five minutes or less. Build some success in from the start and pick a fifteen-minute increment. If you nail that fifteen-minute increment 90 percent of the time for three months, then you can think about reducing it to something like twelve minutes.

This new approach to time will certainly feel foreign to a lot of people when they first try it. But the only reason it seems foreign is because it hasn't become a habit yet. You *can* do this, and when you do you'll immediately see the benefits of attacking the open space.

You've certainly seen that person at your office who is always the one grinding it out late into the evening, long after everybody else has gone home. Heck, you might even *be* that person. This is obviously no knock on working hard, but if you're able to intentionally deal with the unaccounted-for time in your schedule during the day, you'll be able to get more work done in fewer hours. You'll be way more efficient, you'll get more done that needs to be done, and you'll be able to go home feeling better about what you accomplished and spend more time with the important people in your life. You can win at the things that are more important than your job. It's a little like being the kid who totally attacks his study-hall time during the school day so that after school he has more time to play with his friends.

Instead of emphasizing time in terms of how long things take, you'll be changing the paradigm to emphasizing productivity.

PRIORITIZE THE PRIORITIES

As you start to build some momentum from attacking the open space, you're probably going to start wondering how to choose what goes into those open spaces. It's a different process than the OTT concept we talked about in Chapter 1, but definitely related.

To be clear, we don't want you waiting until open time shows up in your day to then start thinking about your "3 Most Important / 1 Must" items. Those things should already be accounted for on your schedule as early in the day as possible.

Attacking the open space is simple. When you find yourself with a few extra moments, ask yourself what is the most *important* thing you can get done with the available open time window. The tasks you will do when you have those extra few minutes are not from the "3 Most Important" list but are other important tasks that you can now fit into your day even though they were not on the primary lists.

Most people in this situation will go to their to-do list and pick one of the easiest, quickest items to complete. Unfortunately, that runs counter to everything we've learned about prioritization. Remember, it isn't about getting everything done. It's about getting the most important things done. When the open space shows up, avoid working on those less important tasks and instead attack the absolute most important item you can get moving on within the time available.

The efficiency you gain by filling the unaccounted-for time is directly tied to how well you choose and prioritize which to-do items go into those spots. When you do it well, you're like an NFL football team with a good game plan and a full week of practice ahead of a big game. If you don't, it's as if you told your team that they'd be playing a game Sunday, but didn't have any details about who the opponent would be, where the game was to be held, or what time it was being played. The second team is pretty much relegated to showing up and winging it. Unfortunately, that's the level where most people play in business.

We teach the students in our seminars to come in with a much more specific plan. They learn to identify and rank their priorities on two scales—the "macro" items and the "micro" ones. The macro scale is the list of categories themselves—prospecting for new clients, emailing, writing proposals, or having meetings with clients.

We believe there are two categories of productive behavior—short-term revenue collection (those activities that produce immediate financial results) and long-term revenue cultivation (the lead activities that eventually bring about a consistent supply of revenue-generating opportunities).

Let's use an analogy. If you were an orange farmer, your short-term revenue collection would be going out and picking the fruit from the trees. The long-term cultivation of revenue would consist of taking care of the trees themselves, planting new trees when necessary, and so on.

Most people in the business world pay plenty of attention to short-term revenue collection activities. However, there's a real weakness when it comes to prioritizing the long-term revenue-cultivation activities. Highly successful people have learned that short-term revenue collection *and* long-term revenue cultivation need to be emphasized daily.

The micro-scale activities are the individual activities within the categories themselves. For example, within the prospecting category, you'd have items such as asking for referrals, or meeting with centers of influence. The key is to start with the most important. Choose your best client to ask for a referral first, then move to your second-best client, and so on. Reach out to your most influential center of influence before making contacts with some of your less-connected influencers.

It's easy to see how it works in a sales-driven job, but the tool is just as applicable in other lines of work. Let's say you're a physician. Along with short-term revenue generation (seeing patients), you might be thinking about the quality of patient interactions. The longer-term cultivation component might be concerned with engaging in ongoing training or meeting with centers of influence that could potentially refer you to new clients.

No matter what category of activity you are operating in, always begin with the most important thing you can do. If you are emailing, return emails to your most important clients or prospects first. If you are completing paperwork, always begin with the most critical documents.

TRIM THE FAT

Working hand in hand with prioritizing is actively reducing the amount of time you spend on things that you need to do.

Schedule bloat is one of the most common—and most irritating—issues facing people who want to become high achievers. In short, it is quite normal to allow certain activities in your day to last longer than necessary, but you can learn not to let this happen.

Spending *more* time on critical activities shouldn't be the main objective. High achievers have learned how to get more done in less time. You should be trying to figure out how to do what you're doing every day more efficiently—and how to make the time you spend on them more in tune with the overall priorities you've been setting.

There are a few methods for making this happen. First, it is essential to set your "game clock." You must predetermine how long you will commit to a certain activity ahead of time. Once you set that game clock, you need to treat it just like the game clocks you would see at a basketball or football game. When the time expires, the game is over, and you need to move on to the next thing on the schedule.

Knowing that you have a time limit should be the first step in getting you motivated to improve your efficiency. The game-clock concept is extremely helpful when you're tasked with organizing a meeting. Instead of telling people in a general way that the meeting starts at 9 a.m., establish a specific time frame for it—9 to 9:25 a.m.

When we set up meetings, we actually make it a point to emphasize twice how long it is scheduled to last—first when the appointment is confirmed, and again right at the beginning of the meeting. It lets people know you plan to honor the clock—and that you respect their time.

Group meetings are always the low hanging fruit in conversations like this. They've become an integral part of the culture and of so many organizations that it's doubtful we'll ever be able to completely get rid of them—and some are obviously necessary. Unfortunately, most corporate meetings are filled with people talking about work instead of actually working.

And virtually every organization does a bad job of really understanding the cost to the business when three, thirty, or three hundred staffers get together for a meeting. We're not saying the cost isn't worth it in some cases—because it certainly is. But when you think about the equivalent hourly pay for everybody at the conference table, and the value of the work they would be doing if they weren't sitting in the meeting, that meeting's opportunity cost is certainly more than a plate of bagels and some cream cheese.

If you're in charge of a meeting, you have a lot of power to improve how that meeting is run. The first question you should be asking yourself is, "Do I really need all the meetings I am scheduling?" Even if there is one ongoing weekly meeting you could eliminate, that would be great progress. Maybe instead of weekly, you could meet every other week. The next step is to think about setting a game clock for each of your regular meetings, and choose one of those to shorten the clock by fifteen minutes from where you currently have it.

When Tom was at American Funds, his rule was that no meeting or conference call could last more than seventeen minutes. He would address one or two major points, outline the necessary action, and then get everyone back to work. Keep in mind that this was well before anyone had heard of TED talks.

Carve the meeting down to its three main elements—an opening, the main purpose, and the closing. In the opening, get right into the meat of what you want to accomplish by asking if anything important has changed since the last meeting. Then quickly transition into the main purpose by declaring the (very) short list of things that have to be accomplished (ideally, this would be one thing, and absolutely never more than three).

When the game clock gets down to five minutes or so, start the transition to the closing by asking, "What are the main takeaways from this meeting, and what is the next step of action?"

Meeting adjourned.

What if there's no action to take? Then you probably didn't need a meeting at all. You could have sent out a memo.

Some quick tips for running effective conference calls:

- Realize going in that "distractions are a given."
- Hook their attention with a quick story or pertinent fact in the first twenty seconds.
- Make one or two points, and keep it simple.
- Know how you are going to finish—before you begin.
- Limit your time to seventeen minutes; anything longer, and the distraction monster is likely to win.

Group meetings are just the most obvious opportunity area. Client meetings and sales calls are other activities in our schedule that potentially eat up large amounts of your time because of the obvious pressure to generate new business.

The goal is to earn new business and to keep existing clients completely happy with less time spent. Many of the individuals we work with have examined their sales meetings and reduced them from an average of sixty minutes down to forty minutes across the board, just by making a few adjustments in how they handle the relationships. Instead of rambling on, in an effort to build a "relationship" with the person across the table from you, approach the interaction the way a college coach would with a basketball player. We call it the "2-1-1."

If it's a client, start the conversation by complimenting two things the client is doing well. Follow that up by teaching the client one thing (within your scope of expertise) that will cause him or her to improve. Lastly, coach the client on a single, action-able element. Your goal with every individual meeting should be to leave the other person motivated to take *action* on something that will improve his or her life. Complimenting the client will deepen the relationship, and teaching the client will increase your credibility, thus leaving him or her motivated to listen and take action on what is offered in the coaching.

This process is very different from trying to become some-body's friend.

We're not suggesting that you run people in and out in an impersonal way—and obviously, this exact format will not work for every kind of one-on-one meeting. But in our view, the "relationship-building" pendulum has swung too far the other way in the business world. The best way to deepen relationships is to actually do your job with the client.

> The best way to deepen relationships
> is to actually do your job with the client.

People like to do business with people they like, but they also like doing business with people who get the job done and don't waste their time. If your financial advisor, mechanic, or brain surgeon came into a meeting and was friendly but didn't make things better for you, how long would it take before you were looking for someone else to work with? As a professional, you have a responsibility to coach your clients to improve on one thing in every single meeting, or you have more than likely just wasted your time and theirs.

This lesson becomes exponentially more important the more you move up the food chain, because the people you will be dealing with will be operating under the same time and scheduling constraints that you're reading this chapter to solve. Small talk is fine at a cocktail party, but it can be irritating when it happens during working hours.

As you use these three tools, it's also useful to remember what Coach Wooden considered to be the most important key to developing a disciplined team.

Start *every* meeting on time. No matter who is meandering in late, reward those who showed up early by beginning on time. The more consistent you are with this rule, the more respect you will earn, and the more people will begin showing up on time for meetings.

FIXING PROCRASTINATION NOW, NOT LATER

With any well-intentioned diet, workout routine, or organizational plan, it's easy to sit in the calm times and plot out the "ideal" way to do things. But, as Mike Tyson famously said about boxing, everybody has a plan until they get punched in the mouth.[1]

Any of the concepts in this book will only work for you if they account for what happens in the real world and give you strategies for overcoming the problems you're going to encounter. Time maximization is no different. Even if you have the willpower and determination of a Navy Seal, you're going to run into times when you don't have the same energy to push and "change time." It's natural, and it's called procrastination. We've all been there.

You see something on your schedule you just don't want to do—either because it's something unpleasant, like a conversation you don't want to have, or because it's complicated and time-consuming, and you know it will take time you don't have at the moment.

And so you keep putting the thing off to later and later in the day, or move it to later and later in the week or month. Maybe you're hoping it will secretly disappear. The reality is that you're trading your time at the moment for time at some point in the future.

It wouldn't be such an issue if each problem we confront every day existed in a vacuum. But work and time and life go on, and when you procrastinate and push things down the road, the things getting pushed join the other things on your plate at the receiving end.

As you get more behind and have more on your plate, you're going to feel stressed, rushed, and out of control. That's when the size of the job at hand—or the pure number of different jobs you have to do—can overwhelm you. It happens every day, and the most common response is paralysis. People get overwhelmed, and they just stop.

One of our favorite ways to attack procrastination is to break those dreaded activities into much more manageable pieces. It's called "ask and chop." You ask yourself, "What is the most important thing I can get done next?" and then you "chop" that activity down into the first step of action.

For example, if you have something to do that you've been avoiding, the first, small step of progress toward completing it will help overcome the "human inertia" we talked about earlier. Instead of allowing your mind to become overwhelmed with the activity in its entirety, emphasize only the first step. Rather than completing the entire monthly expense report, just get the first day noted. Attacking the first step of action creates confidence and puts you on the productive side of action.

Something about chopping the activity up into smaller pieces seems to free people from many of the stalls that keep them from making progress.

One of Jason's hockey clients leaned on this technique almost exclusively to get into peak shape during one off-season and earn a lucrative contract extension. The player had never been very motivated when it came to working out, but had always compensated for a relative lack of fitness by being very well prepared mentally and strategically. He was a great "clubhouse guy," beloved by his teammates and coaches, but injuries had slowed him down for a few seasons, and his strength and conditioning had become much more important.

After meeting with Jason one spring, the player decided that he needed to build another forty minutes into his physical training routine. But instead of letting his mind focus on all of the additional work, he would tell himself, "I'm just going to focus on getting one set done." Instead of adding the forty extra minutes onto the end of his current routine, he decided to "chop" it up. He would do one set here and one set there. It worked, because completing just one set felt so much easier than adding forty extra minutes per day into his already packed schedule.

The player came into camp in the best physical shape of his career and was able to play more minutes per game than he ever had. After a strong regular season, he played even better in the playoffs. The team rewarded him with a three-year contract extension—a payoff both in money and in the opportunity for his young son to become old enough to really understand and enjoy his dad playing professional hockey. The father-son experience was literally priceless to our client.

To beat procrastination and create inertia toward time maximization, remember to "ask and chop."

The Big Why: The more successful you become, the smaller the unit of time you must think in.

The Inversion Test: The average income in the United States is around $50,000 annually. The goal is to be much better than average. To do so, you must begin thinking in smaller units of time. Most people think in time periods of one week. Mondays are dreaded, Wednesday is hump day, and then there's TGIF. Allowing yourself to think in longer units of time will cause you to get less of the most important work completed—costing you money and self-confidence. You will be busy but not very productive. Thinking in smaller units of time will enable you to maximize your time. That doesn't mean you will be "busier," but you will be more productive.

> Thinking in smaller units of time will enable you to maximize your time. That doesn't mean you will be "busier," but you will be more productive.

Act Now: Take a sticky note in your office and write down your Time Maximization "Open Space" Number. This is the number of minutes, between one and fifteen, that will become your default trigger for knowing you need to get at least one thing productive completed when unaccounted-for time appears.

Some examples from our clients:

PRO ATHLETE
Time Maximization "Open Space" Number is 10 minutes. Anytime that 10 minutes or longer of open space shows up between 1:30 p.m. and game time, I will commit to getting at least one set of armband exercises done to keep my shoulders and elbows strong.

FINANCIAL ADVISOR
Time Maximization "Open Space" Number is 8 minutes. Anytime that 8 minutes or longer of open space shows up between 8:30 a.m. and 4:00 p.m., I will reach out to one potential prospect. This could include reaching out to a current client or client of interest and asking for a referral if I don't have an identified prospect to contact.

LAWYER
Time Maximization "Open Space" Number is 5 minutes. Anytime that 5 minutes or longer of open space shows up during office hours, I will check my most important in-progress file and note if any action needs to be taken in the next 24 hours.

4

WIN YOUR
FIGHT-THRUS

Joe Berger, a client from the business world, came to us with a very common story.

He was producing terrific sales numbers, but the way he was going about it was producing a tremendous amount of stress. He also knew he was leaving a lot on the table every month.

Joe would have some incredible, record-setting sales months, but they would inevitably be followed by months with very poor numbers. And his attitude certainly matched where he was on the sales dial. In the great months, he felt like he was on top of the world. But in the slow months, stress and anxiety would consume him to the point that it affected his home life, health, and diet.

What had always eluded Joe was *consistent* high achievement. Simply put, Joe was a professional rider on the roller coaster of success. He didn't have the habits that would push him through and keep him on the high plane of success and make the lows less low.

After some consultation, Joe embraced the concept of the "fight-thru," a strategy we're going to talk about in this chapter. Once he learned how to win many of the small battles within himself day to day, everything changed. His normal routine of up and then down was replaced by consistent performance and gradual improvement.

In the past two years, Joe's business has increased more than 40 percent, and he's lost 40 pounds by avoiding the binge stress eating he used to do. The changes have been so stark that the other people in his group at work named a scale of improvement after him—the Berger Scale of Success, a combination of weight lost and percentage points of business increased.

It all came from learning to "fight-thru," and it's something anybody can do—with some practice.

The entire subject of habits—how they're formed, how long it takes, how easy or hard they are to break—is shrouded in misunderstandings and misrepresentations of the work of one man: Dr. Maxwell Maltz, who presented his ideas in his 1960 book *Psycho-Cybernetics.*[1]

You've probably heard that it takes something on the order of twenty-one consecutive days of the same intentional activity to create a habit. That's something that was pulled out of Maltz's book and oversimplified to the point where it is far from the point he intended to make.

Maltz wasn't even talking about habit formation when he introduced the time period of twenty-one days. He was talking about patients who had gone through facial surgery, and the amount of time it took them to change their self-images enough to be used to seeing their new faces. His point was that it took a *minimum* of twenty-one days for an established mental image to be replaced with a new one.

Of course, folks with bad habits in 1960 were just like all of us with bad habits today. They really, really wanted it to be as simple as grinding out twenty-one days without a cigarette, or following a new exercise routine or a different diet, desperately hoping that this magic number would enable them to make a lasting change. Unfortunately, it isn't quite that simple.

The reality is that our habits aren't so much formed as they are in a constant state of formation. They're either getting stronger or getting weaker, based on how much attention and reinforcement they're getting each day.

> The reality is that our habits aren't so much formed as they are in a constant state of formation.

If you're looking for the technical answer, researchers from University College London followed one hundred people for twelve weeks as they attempted to establish one new habit—which ranged from something as simple as incorporating a different food into a daily diet to something as ambitious as starting a long-distance running plan. The study revealed that it took the participants anywhere from two and a half weeks to three and a half months to establish their habits to the point where they did the new thing at least 95 percent of the time.[2]

Of course, the devil is in the details.

The factors that impacted how long the habit formation took? According to the study, it depended on how much time someone spent working at the new habit, what the habit was, and how different it was from the person's regular routine. In other words, there is no magic twenty-one-day "cleanse" that will spit you out the other side stronger, thinner, or with more oxygen in your lungs.

But before you get discouraged, there *is* a process you can follow to develop a set of habits (or regular practices) that will serve you well in your professional and personal life. It's a matter of following some simple steps that work in concert with how your brain functions—not against it.

In basic terms, behavior patterns or habits start in the same part of the brain as the one responsible for memories and emotions. There's an external trigger for the habit, the behavior itself, and then the emotional response to the behavior. When you respond to the trigger with the behavior, and the behavior makes you feel good, it reinforces itself into a habit loop. Over time, that loop becomes an ingrained part of your brain's "programming," to the point that the habit activity happens almost without conscious thought.

Whether you're trying to add a new, good habit to your daily routine or replace a bad one with something else, you're going to go over the same "mental terrain." Our goal here is to give you a roadmap to that terrain, so that when you get to it, you aren't surprised by what you see and feel, and you have a guide to help you push through it.

We separate that guide into three different phases—the honeymoon, the fight-thru, and second nature. The mere act of recognizing the phases of habit formation when you see them and calling them out to yourself is a huge positive step, and it will provide a major boost in energy.

> The mere act of recognizing the phases of habit formation when you see them and calling them out to yourself is a huge positive step, and it will provide a major boost in energy.

THE HONEYMOON

This is a neighborhood we all know very well. You've decided to start a new, regular routine at gym, or keep your desk much more organized, or set up a system so that your client information always gets updated in a central place.

It usually happens because of some kind of jolt—either positive or negative. Maybe you went to a conference and heard a talk that really inspired you, or you lost an extremely important piece of paper in the mess and missed an important deal. Either way, a "triggering incident" produced plenty of fuel to kick off the habit drive.

And the first few days, it might even be easy. After that first vigorous workout in your new routine, you might say to yourself, "Oh yeah, I can do this. I'm ready for the challenge."

We chart it by email every time we hold one of our training seminars. The students have follow-up access by email for any questions or comments they might have, and our mailboxes fill up the next week like clockwork—with messages about how easy it was to make all the changes, and about how they are already way ahead of the pace we suggested in the program.

But all honeymoons eventually come to an end, and the day-to-day reality sets in.

On day three or day eight or day eighteen, you'll meet one of the constant stream of obstacles that will test your resolve. You'll be presented with many different versions of the same question. Will you take the easier route and go back to "normal," or will you win your "fight thru"?

THE FIGHT-THRU

This is the point where "I can do this" turns into "This is harder than I thought," or, "Is it really going to matter if I miss a day?" To make it through to the third phase, when the habit becomes second nature, you need to be able to win two or three of these important fight-thru battles with yourself.

Here are the four techniques you will need to do just that.

1. Ritualize

The less you leave up to chance (or procrastination), the better your chances are for success. Ritualize the new habit by scheduling it on purpose at the same time every day. If the habit is getting a thirty-minute run in every day, block it out on the calendar for the same time and make it nonnegotiable. Doing it this way takes most of the thinking out of doing it. You're almost automating the process. Over his years at UCLA, Coach Wooden built a dedicated set of rituals that put him where he needed to be each day—from his 5:30 a.m. walk, to meeting with assistants immediately after practice to formulate the plan for the next practice, to finding his wife, Nellie, in the stands before a game and making eye contact.

2. Recognize

As we mentioned above, just the act of recognizing the barrier in front of you is a huge step toward getting over it. When it gets to be day three of the exercise plan and you're lying in bed debating with yourself about whether or not you want to go out in the rain and get it done, recognize where you are. Learn to simply say to yourself, "I've entered a fight-thru." Recognizing that you are in a "fight-thru" is like taking the blindfold off before the fight begins. Now you know what you're fighting. Remind yourself that "It's important to win this one, today." Why? Because each fight-thru win makes the next fight-thru easier to beat, thanks to momentum. Momentum works the other way, too. Each fight you lose makes it easier to quit the next time.

3. Ask Two Questions

As you push through the fight-thru, coach yourself up with two "perspective" questions. Ask yourself how you will feel if you win the fight-thru, and, conversely, ask yourself how you will feel if you lose it. You're taking the next step past recognizing the facts of the situation and bringing emotion into the equation—which is the most valuable kind of fuel. Emotion promotes action. If you've committed yourself to a workout routine, for example, and you hit one of the inevitable fight-thrus, ask yourself the two questions. The first would be, "How will I feel if I win this fight-thru?" Chances are, if you find the strength to win, you will end up feeling like a world champion (even if only for a short period). The second would be "How will I feel if I lose this fight-thru?" If you lose the battle—it will probably bring out the negative emotion that comes with underperforming. Using these positive and negative emotions can help propel you through.

> Emotion promotes action.

4. Life Projection

Take thirty seconds and think, in great detail, about where you think your life will be in five years if you're able to make this change and consistently win your fight-thrus. This is the time to be totally honest with yourself, and really let yourself feel the positives of doing that different thing. Do it in tandem, and go through the same process while thinking about your quality of life if you allow yourself to lose fight-thrus for the upcoming five years. Again, picturing as much detail as you can is really important for maximum effectiveness. The more emotion you bring into it, the better.

The amazing things that world-class athletes are able to accomplish are usually chalked up to freak physical ability—and that certainly can be a factor. But a much bigger factor in those athletes reaching that level is their relentless ability to consistently win the fight-thrus.

Greatness is predicated on consistently doing things others can't or won't do. Simply put, success is *not* about being brilliant. It is about being consistent.

> Greatness is predicated on consistently
> doing things others can't or won't do.
> Simply put, success is *not* about being brilliant.
> It is about being consistent.

The first time we met one of our baseball clients, he was bouncing around in the minor leagues. He was extremely talented, but in six years of pro ball, he had spent less than a full season at the major league level. He knew he was just a few good habits away from a permanent stay in the big leagues, and he came to us for help.

The first habit he needed to incorporate was to control his drinking. He was in no way out of control, but drinking represented a huge component of his social life. He'd finish a game and go somewhere to unwind with "a few" beers, and he'd eat dinner late and stay out socializing. He wouldn't get home until the early morning hours, and the next night he'd do it all over again.

It sounds like something your mother would tell you, but he really wasn't getting enough sleep. He woke up late and groggy, and would usually scarf down some fast food in his rush to the ballpark for a game. He would get to work feeling stressed and underprepared, and it certainly leaked into his performance on the field.

By making a basic habit change and committing to drinking no more than three beers on a night before a game, he self-limited his time out. This started a chain reaction of positive events— more sleep, more time in the morning, a healthier breakfast, and a more relaxed and focused attitude at the park.

Now that he had more time to prepare before games, the player decided to adopt another one of the rules we teach. He committed to getting to the field and spending specific time getting himself mentally prepared to play, using the Mental Workout we're going to talk about in Chapter 6.

He also committed to spending ten minutes before every game doing what is called "deep practice"—training at full speed. One of the player's weaknesses was pitch recognition. Major league players have just a split second to diagnose what kind of pitch is being thrown and decide whether or not to swing. If you don't go in with some kind of game plan about the pitches you expect the pitcher to throw, and have some idea what the spin looks like for each, you're guessing—and you aren't going to be very successful. The player spent ten minutes standing in with the pitchers during their warm-ups, practicing calling out what pitches they were throwing. His goal was to get three in a row correct before the ball hit the catcher's mitt. If he didn't get three in a row, he had to go another round.

The changes he was making were great, but it still took almost a full season of habit development to get them to be a real, inte-grated part of his routine. He would be the first one to say that it took a huge number of fight-thrus to get there.

The first week he made his commitment to limit drinking, one of his best friends on the team celebrated a birthday. After the game, they all went to the bar to celebrate, and the player finished three beers in the first hour. He was thinking about ordering a fourth, but he recognized that he was in the middle of one of those fight-thrus. He forced himself to think about what would happen if he ordered another drink. He realized his "one more" would probably turn into six more. He pictured getting home at three in the morning, and also imagined what he would feel like when he got to the park the next day. It was not a pretty picture.

He ordered another beer, but he made it a nonalcoholic one, and spent another hour celebrating with his buddy before going home and getting to bed before 1:00.

The reality, of course, is that you won't win every time. We're all human, and willpower is imperfect. Four months into his commitment, the player went to a teammate's wedding and completely lost control, drinking hard and deep into the night. It began a two-week cycle where he returned to the habits that had kept him in the minors in the first place. Even though it was the off-season, he still had responsibilities: he had to keep himself in great shape and be ready for spring training.

The key was that after those two weeks, the player realized that it was getting easier and easier to lose those internal willpower fights, and he didn't like where he was or where he was headed.

He made himself imagine where he was going to be in five years if he kept allowing himself to fall off the wagon. He was certain that the remainder of his career would be a series of disappointments and underperforming. The thought of never reaching his potential haunted and disturbed him. He learned to use the negative emotion to help recommit himself to his original goals, and doing so caused him to start winning fight-thrus again.

When spring training came, the player was ready. He had his best spring, and he made the big league team. He hasn't seen a minor league field in three years—he has become a full-time major league starter.

SECOND NATURE

After you've won a series of fight-thrus (both big and small), you'll start to enter that "getting into the groove" phase that feels so good. The new habit has become a regular part of your routine, and doesn't feel so much like something you have to intentionally remember or push yourself to do.

It's a great place to be, but you also need to keep your guard up to protect against some really common traps that can send you back to the fight-thru phase. These traps are the reason business professionals don't repeat strong results year over year, ex-smokers become smokers again, and writers never get that first novel completed.

The Discouragement Monster

One of the unfortunate realities of the world is that just because you work hard and do the right things, good things don't *automatically* flow to you. Life can happen in streaks and slumps, and it can be incredibly discouraging if you put in the work to change an important habit and it does not immediately produce the benefits you expect. Maybe you changed a key way you interact with potential clients, and it hasn't yet produced the numbers you expected. Or you changed your diet and it didn't produce the weight loss you hoped. It is very easy to slip into the mindset of *"Why do I bother? It doesn't matter what I do anyway."* The discouragement

monster, as we call it, is so dangerous because it saps your willingness to keep trying. You must remember that scoring often comes
in spurts.

> The discouragement monster, as we call it, is so
> dangerous because it saps your willingness to keep trying.
> You must remember that scoring often comes in spurts.

Disruption

It happens every single year. Just before summer, millions of
people start a new diet and exercise routine and get into a great
pattern. It's going well, and November comes around. They get
knocked off track by Thanksgiving, and in a couple of weeks the
Christmas party circuit starts. By January, they're right back where
they were in June. It can happen a million other ways as well. You
might get sick, go on a long vacation, or even take a weekend and
put work out of your mind. Whether it's vacations, illnesses, or
holidays, any break in the routine is a potential disruption. And
any of those disruptions can put a major dent in your positive
habits.

Seduction of Success

Maybe the most dangerous of the three comes when you actually
have great success with the new habit. You've won the fight-thrus,
you've changed your pattern, and now you're really humming
along. It's absolutely human nature to get to that point and think—
even for a second—*"Hey, I've got this licked. I've figured it out, and I
don't have to work quite as hard now that I have it down."* Then you

---

test that new theory, and lo and behold, the results still show up for a short while. You allow yourself to believe you're the special one who won't have to work as hard as the others to produce results. You know what happens next. You punch another ticket for a ride on the success roller coaster. A few years ago, we worked with a successful college baseball pitcher who was as talented as any athlete we'd ever seen. He pushed himself in training, and he was relentless in his throwing program. He aced his process goals, every day. He got drafted, and quickly worked his way up to the major leagues. After his first full season, though, he started to gradually tail off with his process goal work. Regardless of what we said, we couldn't get him to realize that he was headed for trouble. He started focusing more on his bank account and the size of his next contract. In three years, he was out of baseball completely. His response to what happened: "The things I did early in my career worked so well, I stopped doing them."

We have another client who is one of the preeminent personal-injury attorneys in the United States. She didn't have any trouble in the courtroom, but at times she struggled with some of the other aspects of the job. Her firm compensated her on how many cases she brought in as well as whether or not she won them.

She had always been passionate about helping clients, but, like many attorneys, she didn't look forward to the part where she had to market herself to new clients. She needed to figure out how to be better at the daily grind of finding potential clients and signing them up.

She determined that she wanted to develop one new habit to get better at that part of her job. To do this, she committed to spending thirty minutes per day writing blog posts for her firm's website. The idea was to expand her profile and start to be recognized more frequently by potential clients.

Most of this attorney's struggles came from discouragement. She told us that the hardest weeks were the ones where she devoted hours of time to making new connections but none of it seemed to bear fruit. She kept feeling like she wanted to quit putting effort into looking for new clients, even though she knew that would only make things worse.

She did have some days that went really well, but those days made her struggle in a different way. Since she didn't enjoy the marketing part of her job, it made her hope against hope that grabbing three or four new clients in a short time would put her in a position where she didn't have to work on the marketing side so hard for a few weeks or months.

The first step toward beating the enemy—and avoiding going back to the fight-thru phase—is to know the enemy. Our client learned to recognize the discouragement monster when it came— as well as the seduction of success. She learned to recognize the beginnings of "seduction" as one of two conversations she found herself having with herself: "I can't get the marketing work done today because . . . " was one of them. The other was "It'll be okay if I don't do it today because. . . . "

Recognizing seduction is such an important part of avoiding it. Anytime you catch yourself saying, "I can't do my most important tasks today because . . . ," or, "I don't need to do my most important activities today because . . . ," you know you are entering the seduction zone.

Recognition is great, but what do you do next?

Anytime you recognize that you're backsliding, choose to do "a little bit more, for a little while." If you are becoming seduced, choose that day to do up to 10 percent more on your "1 Must." Doing just a bit more even for that one day will bookmark in your mind the fact that you have the ability to win fight-thrus.

If you are becoming seduced, choose that day to do up to 10 percent more on your "1 Must." Doing just a bit more even for that one day will bookmark in your mind the fact that you have the ability to win fight-thrus.

For example, when our client started feeling pretty good about her marketing work, to a point of thinking she might take the day off on the blog posts, she committed to three extra minutes writing that day. It isn't that writing for three extra minutes (or doing any other habit-related task for a few minutes) will have a huge impact on your results. That isn't the point of doing it. You're reminding yourself during that extra time that you're willing to put in the extra work, and that you're mentally strong. That you're different from other people. When "normal" people experience success, they have a tendency to respond by doing a little less. When mentally tough people experience success, they stay totally committed to what caused the success. It's amazing what that kind of thinking can do for your overall attitude!

When "normal" people experience success, they have a tendency to respond by doing a little less. When mentally tough people experience success, they stay totally committed to what caused the success.

If you do fall into one of those traps, it isn't the end of the world. It's like going back to driver education school after you get a collection of speeding tickets. You go back to the fight-thru phase and win some more of those to earn your place back in second nature.

The overall win is the commitment to pushing past the fight-thru phase no matter how many times you have to go back to it. Remember, every time you win a fight-thru, the next one gets easier to win.

> Remember, every time you win a fight-thru,
> the next one gets easier to win.

That's not to say the process is going to be easy or pain-free. If you want to be extremely successful, you have to commit to doing things that many people aren't willing to do. If it was easy, everybody would do it. But just like physical training makes your body strong, perseverance and willingness to relentlessly fight thru the obstacles make you mentally strong.

It is the training ground for mental toughness. You're establishing winning as a habit.

"PUKE-A-LICIOUS" WORKOUTS

One of our NHL clients showed us just how powerful the "a little more for a little while" concept can be. This player was one of the top players on his team, and the team had done so well they had qualified for the playoffs with three weeks to go in the season.

When that happened, the coaching staff got everyone together and told them to lay off their strength and conditioning training, so they would have "fresh legs" once the postseason started.

Our client was young and strong, and one of his "3 Most Important" items was to get four additional strength and conditioning workouts in every week. He wanted to listen to his coaches, so he stopped doing the workouts—and promptly found himself playing the worst hockey of his career going into the final days of the regular season.

After talking to the coaches and getting permission to get back onto his workout routine, the player decided to make one modification. During one of the workouts, he would push himself harder, for just a few minutes—to the point where his mouth started watering and he was about to vomit.

When we asked him why he did it, he quickly answered, "It's in those puke-a-licious moments that I'm reminded how much of a badass I really am."

In those extra, intense workouts, the player was bookmarking in his mind that he was different. While other players were worn down, or were taking it easy at the end of the season, he was staying committed and even doing more. He was reminding himself that he was growing stronger as the season wore on.

This experience had a huge impact on his confidence, and he's now considered one of the top two-way players in the game.

The Big Why: Habit formation is more than a twenty-one-day set-and-forget process. Life is a constant state of fluctuating habits.

The Inversion Test: Learning to win one fight-thru makes it easier to win the next fight-thru. Losing one fight-thru makes it easier to lose the next, too. If you want to stop making progress, do not put effort into winning your fight-thrus.

Act Now: Learn to recognize what's happening. Write down on a piece of paper one fight-thru you are currently experiencing.

Some examples from our clients:

PRO ATHLETE (THIRTEEN DAYS AFTER THE SEASON ENDS)

I do not want to start my off-season training. I want to relax. I had a great season last year and I am feeling unmotivated about getting things going for the upcoming year. Even though my trainer is on me and I know I need to get going, I am thinking about putting it off for another week.

Winning the Fight-Thru: I reminded myself how I will feel on day one of OTA's (organized team activities) if I don't come in feeling at the top of my game. I have had years before where I started the season not in my best shape, and those years are not the years I want to repeat. The other side of it is when I show up in the best shape of my career: it feels great, my confidence is high, and it always causes me to have a strong start to the season. For me, a strong start is very, very important.

FINANCIAL ADVISOR

I just had my best month ever and I am feeling really strong. I find myself thinking about my results and thinking that maybe, just maybe, I will not have to keep pushing so hard. Even though it only takes about an hour each day to complete my "1 Must" of proactively calling three clients and one prospect per day, I am coming up with excuses to let myself off the hook.

continues

Winning the Fight-Thru: I remind myself that the single most important reason I had such a strong month last month was because I made my proactive contacts daily—no excuse. I know I need to continue this and I force myself to realize that "process guarantees results . . . good and bad." If I follow a bad process, I will have poor results. It's that simple.

PHYSICIAN

I have been staying up late watching the NBA playoffs. I played college basketball and I love watching the big guys hoop. When my alarm goes off at 5:00 I know I need to get up if I am going to have time to get my workout in. Problem is, I am just too tired, and I know I need more sleep if I am going to be sharp for my patients.

Winning the Fight-Thru: I've lost ten to twelve pounds over the past six months and I feel really good about doing so. I know if I keep giving myself a pass on making my workouts, it will be just a matter of time before the lost weight comes back. If I am going to get up at 5:00, I know I need to get at least seven hours of sleep for my mind to be sharp. I need to begin setting a "lights-out curfew" for myself no later than 9:45 p.m. each night. I can record the games and watch them commercial-free the next morning while I work out. If pro-athletes set lights-out curfews, I guess I should be approaching my performance the same way.

HALFTIME

In sports, the halftime break gives coaches a chance to evaluate what has happened so far and come up with a plan for the rest of the game.

Our goal is for you to do much more than just read this book. We want you to *use* it and to incorporate the things you've read into your everyday life. Remember, knowing something doesn't change your life. Doing something does.

So, just like the coaches at halftime in a game, we're going to go through what's happened so far, pull out the most important takeaways—and then make a plan for what's coming up.

Below, we've made a list of what we think the three main ideas are from each of the first four chapters. It's by no means set in stone—if you took something else to be the most important concept, we're not telling you you're wrong. For you, maybe that is the most important thing at this point in time.

Either way, you now have a new assignment. Pick one of the ideas below—or the different idea you identified to be the most important—and go back to the chapter describing it. Reread the information pertaining to that idea to get it more firmly set in your mind.

Once you've done that, find a friend, colleague, or family member and explain the concept to that individual. In one of the most influential educational studies ever published, French researcher Jean-Pol Martin established that students who taught their peers the French language gained much more command of the material than students who learned conventionally from professional teachers or strictly studied on their own. The act of preparing to teach the information, presenting it, and interacting with others who were learning it both enhanced the learning process and increased learning speed.[1]

In simple terms, when you teach something effectively to somebody else, you are effectively learning it at a much deeper level.

OUR TOP 3 TAKEAWAYS: CHAPTERS 1–4

CHAPTER 1:
ORGANIZE TOMORROW TODAY

1. If you prepare successfully, you're preparing yourself to succeed.
2. Writing down your goals (3 Most Important / 1 Must) for the next day engages your subconscious mind in problem-solving while you sleep.
3. Don't mistake "busy" for "productive."
4. _____

   _____

CHAPTER 2: CHOOSE WISELY

1. Choose wisely what you commit to—overcommitting is common and has a very negative impact.

2. Respect channel capacity.
3. Focus on "1 step" and you will have much more success crossing the finish line.
4. _____
   _____

CHAPTER 3: MAXIMIZE YOUR TIME

1. The more successful you become, the smaller the unit of time you should be thinking in.
2. Attacking the open space, prioritizing the priorities, and trimming the fat are all effective methods of *creating* more time.
3. Once you've identified that thing, "chop it" by separating out the first action step you can take on it.
4. _____
   _____

CHAPTER 4:
WIN YOUR FIGHT-THRUS

1. Habits are in a constant state of formation.
2. The most essential step of winning a "fight-thru" is being able to recognize when you've entered a fight-thru.
3. Every time you win a fight-thru, it makes it easier to win the next one.
4. _____
   _____

5

EVALUATE CORRECTLY

Tom was a twenty-five-year-old high school basketball coach when he got his first chance to coach in college. The team he took over had been historically bad—with twenty-one losing seasons in a row. In Tom's first week on campus, the football coach came by his office to meet the new guy.

"Do you have any idea what a mess you're getting yourself into?" he asked.

Tom replied that he did, and set out to prove that the mess could be cleaned up. He was going to use the basics that John Wooden had established with his teams—a focus on fundamentals and conditioning.

Tom put his team members through an intense off-season conditioning program, having them run miles and miles in distance training, and following that up with brutal wind-sprints backward and forward up the big hill on campus.

When it came time to practice at the start of the season, the players were in the best shape of their lives. Tom and his assistant then began the exhausting process of establishing a set of common fundamentals in every player—starting all the way back at the beginning, with how to hold the ball, and graduating to passing and shooting skills.

With constant coaching and review, it took more than a month to establish the necessary work ethic, and another month to get some of the new skills ingrained. The players—and the coaches—were excited to put their improvements to the test under game conditions. But in the first eight games of the season, the team only won one game—even though they had run out to double-digit leads in six of them.

After the seventh loss, Tom was sitting in a dingy little hotel room in the middle of nowhere, replaying every game in his head and trying to figure out the missing piece. In one game, against Central Arkansas (National Basketball Association Hall-of-Famer Scottie Pippen's alma mater), his team was up 18 points before halftime, only to let the lead slip away in the second half. And Tom had an epiphany: he realized that his players now had the ability, skills, and work ethic to execute, but when they were presented with adversity—the other team making a run—they folded.

So Tom made an adjustment. Every night, after practice, he had each player on the team go through a mental exercise. He asked the players to take one minute to think about one thing they did right during that day's practice or game.

The positives from that simple act of self-evaluation and self-encouragement grew almost immediately. Over the next fourteen games, the team went 6–8 while they integrated the new routine. Then, over the last six games of the season, they went 5–1. They were beginning to be considered one of the toughest teams in the conference.

The next year, with the same core group of players, the team went 20–5, the basketball program's first winning season in twenty-three years.

———

The athletes and business leaders we train in our practice and seminars all have different goals they're trying to reach and issues they want to learn to deal with, but there are a surprising number of common threads in the conversations we have. And those conversations would almost certainly be familiar to you, too.

Whether you're a professional athlete, an analyst at a brokerage firm, or an IT manager at the company down the street, you're trying to work your way from where you are to the next rung on the success ladder. Performance is obviously the main driver, and evaluation is a critical tool. If you don't have an accurate picture of how you're doing—and a way to use that information to move you forward—you're flying blind. Asking yourself what you're doing well and what you want to improve is the first step of positive growth.

> If you don't have an accurate picture of how you're doing—and a way to use that information to move you forward—you're flying blind.

Virtually all of the successful people in any endeavor have the same basic "emerging pattern." See if this sounds familiar.

When you first achieve some success, you begin to have the expectation that you'll continue to be successful. If you're a salesperson and you smash your boss's goals for year one and get plenty of accolades, you're almost certainly going into year two with more confidence than you had before and a built-in expectation that you're going to do even more.

Athletes are the same. When the highly touted recruit comes in and plays right away as a freshman and has success, everybody starts projecting out what will happen in the future. Will he come back and play another year? Will he turn pro? They're projecting that the player will continue to shine and improve at the same rate, and it becomes a given in the player's mind as well.

This expectation of improvement is where the seeds of the "perfectionist mentality" are planted. Thoughts of, "Yeah, I did a really good job" are quickly replaced with, "Yeah, but I could always do better." When you're on that path of early success, you're building a constant elevation of perfection into your measurement of success and failure. You tend to write off your success as "I expect that of myself" and focus relentlessly on your shortcomings.

We're not here to criticize that effort and openness to learning and improvement. What we're concerned with is the tendency to overlook those things you are already doing well. Evaluation is the genesis of improvement, however if the evaluation isn't done correctly it will be counterproductive. Unfortunately most people learn to evaluate with the perfectionist mentality.

> Evaluation is the genesis of improvement, however if the evaluation isn't done correctly it will be counterproductive. Unfortunately most people learn to evaluate with the perfectionist mentality.

There's a big problem with the perfectionist pattern. It works great at the lower levels of achievement, when natural talent and a strong drive will let you fix your mistakes, and when you can make gains relatively easily by outperforming and outworking the competitors in your immediate circle. But what happens as you move into more competitive arenas? When you move from the minor leagues to the big leagues, or from the regional office to the national office?

When the pool gets deeper and there is less separating you from the others in your group, you're going to have a harder time "winning" as often.

At the lower levels of competition, the perfectionist mentality isn't as damaging because there are so many external pats on the back available for solid performances. But as the level of competition increases it becomes more difficult to feel good, because those external pats on the back happen much less often.

You see it in the NFL all the time. A player who was able to freestyle and make plays with athleticism and field vision in college gets swallowed up when all the other players on the field are elite, too, and playing within a well-designed system. The level of play is so high that it becomes much harder to stand out.

There just isn't as much room to win on pure talent or determination anymore, and it becomes natural to experience more failure than you're used to.

When the level changes like that, the perfectionist method of evaluation becomes completely ineffective and often unhealthy. If your personal sense of measurement and worth is based on wins and losses and *always* doing better, what do you think happens when you aren't winning as often?

If you aren't evaluating yourself in a productive way, the losses and "failures" erode your self-confidence. When you aren't as confident, you can't perform as well. This causes you to fail more often—starting a vicious cycle. Let's be clear: this isn't the "everybody should get a medal" mentality. Quite the contrary, we are not asking you to feel good about things you haven't done or achieved. Rather, we want you to learn to simply give credit where it's due. Most people spend great time and energy focusing on the things they didn't accomplish while totally overlooking all the things they did accomplish.

> If you aren't evaluating yourself in a productive way,
> the losses and "failures" erode your self-confidence.
> When you aren't as confident, you can't perform as well
> and you fail more often—starting a vicious cycle.

The problem resides in the fact that ultimately one cannot control "winning." By focusing on things you cannot control, you minimize your emphasis on what you *can* control.

It happens to even the most talented athletes and businesspeople in the world—which means nobody is immune. To beat it, you have to learn the art of *performance* evaluation. Using the techniques we're going to be talking about here, you replace those perfectionist tendencies with what we call the "performance mentality."

Instead of burying yourself in negative thoughts and emotions, you will learn how to make effort and improvement (not perfection) your main priority, which in turn gives you the greatest possible potential for impacting results.

THE PERFORMANCE MENTALITY

One of our hockey clients had come into the NHL as a highly touted prospect, but after three seasons he was still trying to live up to his potential. He certainly wasn't a bust—he was getting regular playing time on his team and was a solid contributor at the relatively young age of twenty-five—but he hadn't blossomed into the star everyone thought he would become. He showed flashes of excellence, but he needed to make some changes to become consistently great.

In one meeting, Jason asked the player to tell him one thing he believed he had done well in the previous two weeks. He didn't answer for a long minute.

Then he said, "I know we've talked about this before, but to be honest, I am not proud of myself for anything. I've been judging myself on my results. When things start going bad, I get discouraged and it just makes me play worse. And when good things do happen, I don't end up working as hard—which causes me to make bad decisions off the ice."

From that point, Jason worked out a plan with him where he would stop listening to what the sports talk radio shows were saying about him, and he would quit looking at his statistics after every game.

He started evaluating himself solely on his effort in that day's practice or game. He came up with his own scoring system based on how he moved his feet, how he attacked loose pucks, and whether the shots he took were high-quality opportunities. It wasn't just a matter of filling up the stat sheet in the traditional ways. After each practice, he would grade himself on a scale of 1 to 10 on effort. During games, he'd do the same thing after every shift. Anything less than a 9 was completely unacceptable.

Slowly but surely, he began to be more physical and active on the ice. Something else was changing as well. He was becoming a happier, calmer person off the ice.

Over the next few years, he began to get more and more attention as one of the NHL's up-and-coming players. And, better yet, he knew that he was in control of that success because he was measuring the right things.

THERE ARE NO SPECIAL PEOPLE . . . ONLY THOSE WHO DESERVE IT

This is another one of those places where we're going to tell you something right up front that might not be the sexiest solution you've ever heard.

There is no magic success pill. Success requires strong and consistent effort, and the act of evaluating yourself on that effort. Most people believe that it takes their best effort on *everything,* and that couldn't be further from the truth. Highly successful people give tremendous attention to the most important activities daily and then do *fairly* well with the rest. Remember from the earlier chapters: it's key to have focused attention on your "3 Most Important" and "1 Must." It's definitely a different mindset than most people have, but once you try it, you'll discover something that will give you all the motivation you need: when you give your best effort to your top priorities, the success that comes to you will be deserved.

That may sound simple, but it's really very profound. When you define success by your effort, anything is truly achievable. And when you consistently work toward your goals—and honestly evaluate that effort—you will begin to deserve the success that comes. When it does, you will feel a tremendous sense of validation that doesn't just come when you make your numbers or achieve certain statistics. You will own that success, and it will become a part of your foundation. You will finally have the ability to control the scoreboard. It won't be something that just happens to you. It will be a part of who you are.

> When you define success by your effort, anything is truly achievable. And when you consistently work toward your goals—and honestly evaluate that effort—you deserve the success that comes.

USING THE SUCCESS LOG FOR SELF-EVALUATION

Sure, it all sounds great. But how do you actually *do* it? How do you build a system of evaluation that not only tells you how you're doing but actually helps you build on the effort you need to be successful?

It starts with establishing the right kinds of goals.

There's no question that results are the main driver of almost everything we do or see in modern society. We're all constantly being evaluated on job performance, earnings, looks—even the type of car we drive. It isn't a big mystery, then, that most people have developed a very strong focus on "results thinking." Process goes out the window, and results are all we think about.

But when the focus is only on results, you aren't necessarily building the actual skills you need to be successful. You aren't really learning the *whys* and *hows* that produce those results, which makes it hard for you to pull yourself out of a slump—and adds pressure you don't need.

Imagine that a sales agent in the middle of a client meeting begins thinking to herself, "I have to close this deal if I am going to meet my quota." She wouldn't have the mental bandwidth to focus on listening to the customer's needs, addressing his concerns, and selling the features of the most appropriate product.

The same holds true for a batter up at the plate. If he's in the box thinking about how he needs a hit to get his average over .300, or to kick in one of the performance clauses in his contract, he's probably going to have the bat on his shoulder as the ball blows by him.

In other words, focusing on results—or the end product—actually makes it *harder* to produce those results, and makes any results you do produce take longer to achieve.

And that's the paradox. A focus on results doesn't produce results. Reformatting your thinking to emphasize the *process* is the only way to effectively set goals that will actually produce the results you want to see.

What are the differences between product- or results-oriented goals and process-oriented goals? Product or results goals are the ones that can be measured on an income statement or seen in your job title. If you want to earn $1 million in commissions next year, that's a product or results goal. If you want to become a senior vice president by the second quarter of next year, that's a product or results goal. Write a novel? Another product goal.

Process goals, on the other hand, are the daily activities that *cause* the desired results or product goal. These will typically be your "3 Most Important / 1 Must" commitments daily. Using the same analogies, a process goal for a person who wanted to earn a certain level of commissions or a job title would be to make a certain number of contacts with high-net-worth clients per day, or to shadow somebody in the comptroller's office one day a week to learn some new things. For an aspiring novelist, it would be setting aside two hours per day of quiet time for writing.

There is no magic formula for setting either kind of goal, as long as you follow a couple of core principles.

First, both kinds of goals need to be completely measurable. What does that mean? In the literal sense, they have to be something you can track, not some gauzy judgment call. Whether you made a call or not is concrete. Whether you were happy or not in a given day? Not concrete, and not measurable—at least for the purpose of this tool.

Athletes tend to get measured annually by their wins, their home runs per year, or the prize money they're awarded. Corporations tend to break goals into quarterly chunks—earnings reports, performance evaluations, and so on. All of those are good examples of measurable results-oriented goals. A measurable process-oriented goal would be, for example, an athlete choosing to spend fifteen minutes per day on film study or a successful

CEO spending thirty minutes researching development opportunities in emerging markets.

Second, it is of utmost importance that you choose wisely when it comes to both product and process goals. Product goals need to be realistically high—not so out of sight that you can miss and have a viable excuse for failing ("It was impossible anyway . . . "). And process goals need to be completely within your control—something you have the ability to do every day.

Setting goals too high and hoping to "get close" is one of the most damaging things you can do to your performance. It gets you in the habit of losing. Set your process goals to a point where you can hit them daily, and you build confidence and your ability to "win" mental commitments in the future. It's not about what you will do on your best days but, rather, what you will be sure to do even on your worst day.

> Setting goals too high and hoping to "get close" is one of the most damaging things you can do to your performance.

The third core principle is where you have to learn to be abnormal. Normal people focus almost completely on product goals. And product goals are fine for spectators or stock pickers. But when you're talking about your own goals, it is the process goals that need to be on the forefront of your mind and at the top of your priority list each day. You need to be tracking process goals at least weekly, and preferably daily.

The highest performers learn to devote much more focus—85 percent, at least—to process goals, and they evaluate themselves on how they do on that scale. The product goal—making a certain number or getting a certain title—is the destination. The process goal is how you get there.

In 2006, Jason started working with one of the St. Louis Cardinals players during spring training. The player was coming off an especially bad season the year before, and he told Jason that he felt like he played very "tight."

Jason asked the player what he thought about when he stepped in the batter's box, and the answer was astounding:

> I'm looking at the Jumbotron and I can't believe what it says I'm hitting—.253 or something. I start thinking to myself that this isn't going to work—and that's when it gets in my head. I can actually feel myself start to tighten and press. It's so hard to stay in control of your emotions and thoughts when you have everybody watching and you're under the microscope.

Jason helped the player start focusing on his preparation and performance process instead of the external results of each at-bat.

At the end of the season, the Cardinals had clinched a play-off spot, and the player had improved his average more than 30 points. He had been a key member of the team all season. This is what he said during his "exit interview":

> I basically had to say "screw it" when it comes to results. I made a point to judge myself on the process. Every day, I followed my routine. Every cut. Every ground ball. No matter what the result, I made myself emphasize the process, and I held myself accountable for doing the work. I stopped looking at results and forced myself to think "process" was the win. In the end, the results speak for themselves. Focusing on process flat-out works.

Another client came to us after a successful career as a television broadcaster. She was transitioning into financial advising, and she wanted to make sure she was putting strong building blocks in place at the beginning of her career.

One of the first habits we helped her establish was to be relentless in attacking her two main process goals every day—contacting two high-net-worth investors, and completing her Success Log evaluations. (We'll describe this tool and supply a log form in a few pages.)

Focusing on the process instead of the results you're getting is a challenging transition for most people to make when they go from a salary job to one that relies on commission for compensation— and our client wasn't immune to that. Early on, there were nights when she went to bed wondering if she was going to be successful at this new career, and how she was going to pay her bills in the short term.

But she forced herself to control her thoughts, to the point where all she would allow herself to focus on was her process goals for the day and the game plan for tomorrow. Did she nail her process goals? And what was she going to do in order to do it again the next day?

After a year on the job, she came back to see us, and she said that the process orientation habit she learned was like a life vest keeping her from drowning in discouragement. As the years went by, our client kept to the same simple strategy. Over time, some of the process goals changed and grew, depending on where she was in her career, but the intention always stayed the same.

Now, she is one of the top-grossing advisors in her office, and she's using her process goals for a completely different function. Focusing intensely on the process allows her to "ignore" the great sales results she's producing and keeps her humble and hungry.

She isn't getting distracted by success; rather, she attacks her process every day to continue her winning ways. She's on track to become one of the few female million-dollar producers in her firm, and she attributes it to what she calls the secret of success—process orientation.

The people in these two examples were extremely high achievers, and it still felt very strange to them to revise how they prioritized their goals. There's no question it will feel foreign to you, too. But it's the proven way to get you to where you want to go. And it all begins with effective evaluation. We have combined a series of evaluation questions into what we call Success Logs to help jump-start consistent improvement. They have been proven to help people win World Series titles, national championships, and Olympic gold medals and to significantly increase business production year over year.

The Success Log provided below will literally train your brain to focus more on your strengths, your effort, and your process. It prompts you to think about your process each day and to set goals for the next day accordingly. Take a look at the log on page 99, and then read on to learn how to use it.

GIVE CREDIT WHERE IT'S DUE

As nice as it would be, life isn't like kindergarten. You don't get a sticker from a generous teacher for drawing an unrecognizable lump with your crayons on a piece of construction paper. All of us are getting judged every day. It's a part of life in the business world. It's something you're almost certainly doing yourself already, as are your peers, supervisors, and competitors.

But one aspect of that kindergarten star system still works the same way it did when you were five years old: rewards encourage

SUCCESS LOG

Knowing something does nothing . . . doing something does. . . .

Name: _____ Date: _____

What did I do well in the past 24 hours?
- _____
  _____
- _____
  _____
- _____
  _____

What is one thing I want to improve in the next 24 hours?
- _____
  _____

What is one thing I can do differently to help make the above-mentioned improvement?
- _____
  _____

How did I do today with my "3 Most Important / 1 Must"?

1 2 3 4 5 6 7 8 9 10

you to keep doing your best. But your kindergarten teacher isn't around anymore, so you need to learn to recognize your own successes.

Teachers give out stars because it makes children feel good about an accomplishment and motivates them to work toward the next task. One of the biggest problems successful people have when they evaluate themselves is that they focus only on the negative. It's something known as "problem-centric thinking." People have an innate tendency to obsess over the things they aren't doing well instead of giving themselves credit for the things they are doing well. From there, the issue is compounded because of expectancy theory: whatever you focus on expands.

In essence, it is totally normal to focus on how you are screwing up; unfortunately, by doing so, you make it more likely that you will screw up even more in the future.

In essence, it is totally normal to focus on how you are screwing up; unfortunately, by doing so, you make it more likely that you will screw up even more in the future.

Many successful people often leave out the part of the evaluation that recognizes the good things they've done. They immediately go to the list of things they aren't happy about and hammer away at those. Instead, we want you to build an evaluation ritual that takes advantage of expectancy theory by increasing confidence and performance. This is where the Success Log comes in: it forces you to focus on what you have done well, asks you to identify one thing you want to improve, and prompts you to pick one thing you can do to improve in that one area. In addition, it trains you to form the habit of evaluating your *effort* (on a 1–10 scale) on your most important tasks daily rather than your *results*. Evaluating yourself through the positive lens builds self-confidence and promotes action. Remember, whatever you focus on *expands*.

That's it. It isn't a laundry list of should-haves and might-haves. The whole process should take you no more than three minutes. Do it during the day—preferably at the same time each day—and it will put you in the best frame of mind to attack the upcoming twenty-four hours. You're building what we call a "performance mentality."

Without the log, your self-evaluations can easily go awry. If you're living in the perfectionist mentality, you might have a tough day at the office, and then sit down to try to analyze what went wrong. There's a real potential to beat yourself up there. You'll not only think about the things you did wrong, but question yourself about how you could have possibly made those kinds of mistakes. The problem with that strategy is that it can put you into a downward spiral. Your focus goes to your faults and the mistakes that led to them, instead of being focused on improvements and solutions.

By identifying your "done-wells" for the day with the Success Log, you're establishing a much more balanced scorecard. Another great way to keep track is to have a scratch pad on your desk and simply make a note each time during the course of the day that you're happy with something you've accomplished.

It can be something substantial, like closing a deal, but it certainly doesn't have to be. It can be as simple as reminding yourself after a call that you asked for the referral and even though you didn't get the introduction, "asking is winning." You want to use enough second-level detail in your description that your Success

Log gives you a specific picture of what you did right: reinforcing the positive action will influence your confidence level in the future. "The call went great" is not as useful to know as what specifically went well on the call: "On the call with Roger, I listened well and used a great analogy to help him understand."

Evaluating what you have done well sets a foundation of mental strength that you will eventually be able to build on. You're setting the building blocks for mental toughness. Building your foundation of mental toughness is just like building a house. If the foundation is weak, the home will crack at the first sign of adversity. If it's strong, the house can weather any storm.

Once you've identified three "done-wells," it's time to pick the one thing you want to improve. Again, you're going to write this down with that second-level detail. The sentence you write shouldn't be designed to bring you down, or be overcritical; it should be an affirmative statement of what you want to do. This isn't about focusing on your screw-ups, but about identifying what you want to do better. For example, you might tell yourself that tomorrow you want to do a better job of making your ten proactive contacts and not stopping until all ten are completed. Then you want to spend a moment identifying what action step you can take to move you in the direction of the desired improvement. The rule might be that you don't let yourself check emails until all ten contacts are made.

Active and positive statements are much more productive than passive and negative ones.

Active and positive statements are much more productive than passive and negative ones.

The last thing you want to write down in your Success Log for the day is a 1–10 rating on how well you did with your three most important scheduled items. Start forming the habit of evaluating your effort each day toward the completion of your priorities. Your mind will actually become trained to prioritize what is most important.

One of Tom's favorite stories about the time he spent with his friend and mentor John Wooden is about how Wooden would evaluate his players during a game. It had nothing to do with the eventual score of the game, or the individual statistics any single player put up. Coach Wooden would watch to see how each player made his cuts from position to position on the court as UCLA ran its offense. If the players were making quick, straight-line cuts, they were doing their job. If they got lazy and made more banana-shaped cuts, they weren't.

"You mean to tell me the greatest coach of all time is watching to see if his players are running banana patterns and doesn't even care about the score?" Tom asked in disbelief.

Coach Wooden responded that winning was certainly important—and he knew that making sure his players were cutting properly was the best way to control the outcome. The ability to make the disciplined and correct cut time after time is purely a question of effort. Coach Wooden figured that if his players were winning on the effort front, the results would take care of themselves.

They did. Over sixteen seasons, Coach Wooden's UCLA teams went 620–147. They won ten national championships—including seven in a row—and produced twelve consensus All-Americans. Four of those championship teams had undefeated seasons, and the Bruins won an unprecedented seventy-five games in a row between 1971 and 1973.

TURNING EVALUATION
INTO ROUTINE

As you get better and better at the evaluation process, you can adapt it to give yourself a very useful running "dashboard" of how you're doing in a given day. You'll be able to perform "mini-evaluations" at regular intervals and be able to take quick action to get yourself back on track if you encounter a problem.

Back when Tom was working as a financial advisor himself, he adapted some of his coaching habits to his new life working at a desk. He built out a daily chart of the calls and tasks he needed to accomplish that was very similar in execution to the practice and game plans he had devised as a basketball coach. On that matrix chart, he included the list of clients he needed to speak to that day along with the topics he needed to address. As he worked his way through the list, he would check off the tasks as they were completed.

But the matrix morphed into much more than a task manager. It became a mini-evaluation instrument. Every time Tom moved from his seat—to get a drink of water, walk down the hall to talk to somebody, anything—he would pause first, look at the chart, and ask himself three quick questions: What have I been doing well? What is one skill I need to improve? What is one thing I can do differently to make the improvement?

Tom would then mark his chart with the improvement goals in the places where he needed it, so that when he got to that step he was primed to do well. Much like Coach Wooden, Tom wasn't allowing himself to assess success with results—whether or not he made the sale. By evaluating with a performance focus, Tom was forcing his mind to emphasize what he could control—his process and effort—and he was doing it through a positive lens rather than allowing his mind to emphasize mistakes.

When done correctly like this, the evaluation process forces growth. The mere act of effective evaluation causes improvement. The evaluation element blends directly into the action phase, so that the two work as alternate footsteps in the same walking pattern. You're evaluating, adjusting, and taking action in real time—when you can actually use the information you're gathering—and you can get back on track quickly if you're off course.

> **The mere act of effective evaluation causes improvement.**

That's something that a vast majority of people—even successful people—never accomplish. They're measuring the wrong output—results instead of effort—or hammering away at the negative instead of reinforcing the positive.

That's not evaluation. It's punishment.

> **They're measuring the wrong output—results instead of effort—or hammering away at the negative instead of reinforcing the positive. That's not evaluation. It's punishment.**

One financial advisor told us a story that has become fairly common since we've been running our training program. He was doing about $500,000 in business, but he had been stuck at that level of production for several years. After hearing about effort-driven evaluation during one of our talks, he mapped out a plan for himself—along with some evaluation metrics.

His goal for the next year was to achieve $700,000 in gross production, and he decided that the three things he needed to do in a given day to make that happen were to Organize Tomorrow Today (Chapter 1), make twelve proactive client contacts, and complete the Mental Workout (which we'll get to in the next chapter). The advisor also decided that he was going to stop looking at the commission summary on his screen, and instead judge his success in a given day by how well he did on those three process goals. If he completed them, the day was a win. If he didn't, it was a loss.

In the midst of all this, the advisor went through a terrible personal tragedy, losing a family member and a close friend in a fire. Reeling, the advisor's first reaction was to push work to the back burner. But after a few days, he saw the three straightforward process goals as simple, concrete steps he could take in a world that was swirling around him. It gave him a sense of control—and even escape—to apply his focus to something other than the terrible event.

On some days, it was all he could do to push his way through the calls and the Mental Workout, and he would leave for home by noon. But as the days went on, he started to heal. The process goals and the act of evaluating himself on his effort offered some needed day-to-day stability.

Six months later, at the end of the year, the advisor knew that he had been able to gain some consistency in how he approached his work day-to-day, and he knew that he had done well on his own self-imposed metrics. Still, the numbers blew him away. He had doubled his gross production, to just over $1 million. And even more incredibly, he had done it while *reducing* the amount of stress he felt over work and the number of total hours he put in at the office. The increased success and reduced stress obviously didn't eliminate the sadness of the loss he experienced in his personal life, but they did help with the healing process.

He was finally in control of his success.

CELEBRATE . . . AND FORGET

When you do successfully evaluate yourself, you will inevitably start to see positive results—and you have to make sure to celebrate those wins. That kind of positive reinforcement helps to change your behavior in the long run.

Think about the most effective ways to discipline a child. You can rule by fear and intimidation, and threaten to punish the child if he or she does something wrong. Or, you can positively reinforce the behavior you *want* to see, by using rewards and praise. Which kind of process do you think the child is going to embrace and follow happily? And which kind is going to need constant policing, and then fall apart when the policing goes away?

Rewarding and reinforcing the good habits makes for a more lasting change than negativity and punishment—and adults need even more of that positive reinforcement than children do! We all are much more ingrained in our habits—both good and bad— than a five-year-old is, and we have a lot more freedom to make bad choices.

The reinforcement is more than just anecdotal. It's chemical.

In Norman Doidge's book *The Brain That Changes Itself*, he describes the chemical reactions that take place in the brain when you receive a reward for a solid effort. The brain releases acetylcholine and norepinephrine, neurotransmitters that sharpen the mental map for performance and significantly increase motivation.[1]

Rewarding yourself for great effort creates a positive cycle of improved performance. You become smarter about how to make improvements, and you are much more motivated to search for and find those methods of increased success.

We're not suggesting that you go out and buy yourself a $200 dinner to celebrate nailing your process goals two days in a row. The accomplishment needs to be meaningful, and the celebration should be relative to the size of the win. When you do get that win, recognize it and celebrate. Relax and get your mind off business for a while.

A common example of an effective reward is that you allow yourself to take a half day on Fridays each week that you totally nail your "3 Most Important / 1 Must" lists. One of Tom's favorite strategies when he reaches a certain milestone is to go "off the grid" for thirty-six hours. He isn't reachable by cell phone during that time, and he refuses to talk about business. It's a time to spend with family and friends and decompress from the day-to-day business race.

When you're able to disconnect for a day or two, you're fresher when you come back, and you're ready to pick up the tools again. Come Monday, you've "forgotten" your success, and you're ready to build it all over again. Remember, the equation for *lasting* success is achieve, celebrate, forget . . .

The Big Why: Self-evaluation is arguably the most effective performance tool you can use—when used correctly. Unfortunately, most people evaluate things they cannot ultimately control, thus causing negativity, discouragement, and a lack of focus on priority activities.

The Inversion Test: The mere act of evaluation, if done properly, causes improvement. Failing to evaluate promotes failure.

Act Now: Take sixty seconds now and write down on paper three things you have done well over the past twenty-four hours. Remember, anything that promotes personal and/or professional health (even one inch of improvement!) qualifies as a "done-well."

Some examples from our clients:

PRO ATHLETE

3 Done-Wells

1. Spent 15 minutes on FaceTime with wife and kids while on the road.
2. Did a nice job of attacking 50/50 pucks . . . won 2 out of 3.
3. Only drank 2 beers after the game.

FINANCIAL ADVISOR

3 Done-Wells

1. Started the day by calling 2 high-net-worth clients.
2. Asked one of my high-net-worth clients for a referral.
3. Didn't get the referral, but reminded myself that "asking is winning."

INSURANCE EXECUTIVE

3 Done-Wells

1. Finished all 3 portfolio reviews.
2. Sent my wife a nice text letting her know I was thinking of her.
3. After an argument with my son, followed up 10 minutes later and apologized for yelling and told him that no matter what, I will always love him more than he will ever know—he smiled when he heard that.

6

LEARN HOW TO
TALK TO YOURSELF

Talk to marathon runners, and most of them will tell you the same story about the stretch between mile 21 and mile 26.

That's where the monsters lurk.

When you get to mile 21, it isn't a question of whether you can physically survive the last stretch. You can. It's a question of whether the mental monsters will find you and convince you otherwise.

Katie Sutton felt like one of those monsters was riding on her back at mile 24. She had come out fast and run sub-seven-minute miles for the first seventeen miles—a terrific pace. She told herself that it was a perfect day, and her body felt terrific. All she had to do was bring it home, and she'd shatter her personal best.

But when she got to mile 24, she felt like she wouldn't be able to run another step. Her lungs were searing with pain, and her legs throbbed with every step. If she was going to make it to the end, she would have to get her mind right and confront the monster that had tightened its grip on her, whispering *you never should have gone out that fast,* and *it hurts too much. . . . You should stop.*

Katie was no stranger to pain. A former competitive distance runner for Texas Christian University (TCU), she had been training for her first marathon after college when she'd started experiencing some strange physical symptoms. She went from running eighty miles per week to barely being able to complete a mile before becoming completely exhausted. After a grueling round of tests, Katie's doctor delivered the terrible news. Katie had breast cancer. But fourteen rounds of chemotherapy, thirty-two sessions of radiation, and two surgeries later, she was pronounced cancer-free.

The cancer was gone, but one of the remnants from the disease was the leftover negative chatter in her head. Katie got back into training, but when she started running the longer distances, those thought monsters would swirl—*You're never going to be the same runner again. . . . Why bother?*

Over time, Katie beat back the monsters with a mental training routine like the one you're going to learn in this chapter. She learned a mental ritual to help her develop her mental toughness and replace the negative thoughts with thoughts emphasizing desire over fear and strength over weakness—*Today I am strong. Today I am healthy. Today I am a beast.* And she gained conviction about conquering the next challenge through visualization. During what we call her "Mental Workout," Katie used segments of visualization to intensely focus on the visceral feeling of success in her next performance—especially pushing hard through the most difficult part of the run.

By channeling the power of her mind this way, she set herself up to defeat the negative thoughts before they even came to her. Instead of having to beat them back and silence them, she established a wall that was difficult for them to penetrate in the first place. She went on the attack, instead of playing defense.

In that brutal moment of mile 24, her only goal was to finish those last three miles. Her mind wanted her to pay attention to the fire in her lungs and the agony in her legs, but Katie knew that the more she thought about the pain, the more the pain would grow.

So she defaulted back to her identity statement: *Today I am strong. Today I am healthy. Today I am a beast.*

She started repeating it, over and over. Katie pushed through to mile 25, where she encountered a steep hill—designed to weed out the weak at the end of the race. Using the visualization technique she had learned from the Mental Workout, she pictured herself charging up the hill and picking up speed as she made it to the crest. As she pictured defeating the hill, she realized that her mind had wandered for a few minutes, and she was already on the downslope, gaining speed.

In the last mile, Katie's speed was back. The pain in her legs was a dull memory, and her lungs opened up into the runner's high she loved so much. The monsters were gone, and she crossed the finish line in her personal best time.

She didn't conquer the marathon with her legs, or with her physical training. She beat it with her mind, and by learning how to talk to herself.

———

The concept of "self-talk" is an old and established one in psychology. Simply put, it's the inner monologue you have with yourself inside your own head about who you are, what you believe, and how you feel about what you're doing.

Unfortunately, it is completely normal for your inner dialogue to have a negative slant. You must remember, beating yourself up verbally often does more damage than physically harming yourself.

You must remember, beating yourself up verbally often does more damage than physically harming yourself.

Self-talk is the voice in your head driving you to put in the extra time on an important project at work. When you're worn out at the end of the day and you want to pick up and finish tomorrow, it's self-talk that rallies you to keep going. Conversely, if you've decided you're going to go to the gym three days a week, and today is gym day, self-talk is the voice in your head you're arguing with in bed as you wrestle over whether or not you're going to get up and go.

At a deeper level, your self-talk represents your *self-image*—the way you see yourself. Ironically enough, Dr. Maxwell Maltz's *Psycho-Cybernetics*—the book that produced so much misunderstanding about the formation of habits—was the same one to first touch on the very important idea of self-image, and how it governs a lot of what people are ultimately able to accomplish.[1]

Maltz's theory about self-image is a simple one. He said that a person will not be able to consistently overperform or underperform the self-image he or she has. In other words, if you fundamentally believe you're an average performer (or a terrific one, or a terrible one), you won't consistently be able to do a lot better or a lot worse than that baseline self-assessment.

Since self-image is determined by what you consistently say to yourself about yourself, you have the power to direct your self-image by directing your self-talk.

Since self-image is determined by what you consistently say to yourself about yourself, you have the power to direct your self-image by directing your self-talk.

We'll say that again, because it is very important: By directing your self-talk, you can direct your self-image.

By building a self-image that represents who you truly are and want to be, you can essentially program yourself to be ready for success. To do it, you need to master two tasks. First, you have to become aware of what you're saying to yourself. Then, you have to commit to stop giving yourself permission to use negative self-talk. Berating yourself—even in a joking manner—doesn't help in any way. It damages your self-image, and we want you to stop doing it, right now and from now on.

THE PCT TRAP

Many people believe that they're at least somewhat at the mercy of their thoughts. Doubt and negativity just pop in from time to time, and sometimes you become obsessed with the problems on your plate. And, they say, there's nothing you can really do except try to ignore those thoughts and wait for them to pass.

But if you think like most people, you will be like most people—average. Mentally tough people know nothing could be further from the truth. If you work on controlling your thoughts, you'll get better at it.

Yes, the human mind's "default" setting is to focus on the problems or weaknesses. The problem with focusing on the problem, though—which is called "problem-centric thought," or PCT—is that most people do it at the expense of considering a solution or personal strengths.

In fact, lots of people are being *trained* into problem-centric thought by mental health professionals or "self-help" guides because of the misguided (but well-meaning) idea that talking about a problem is akin to making your problems go away.

Unfortunately, there's no empirical evidence to show that idea actually works. Just talking about a problem—and moving your problem-centric thinking to the forefront—doesn't do anything to solve that problem. Actually, it usually just makes the problem grow in size, thanks to something called "expectancy theory."

It goes like this: When you focus on something, it literally occupies the forefront of your mind. Other thoughts and ideas are pushed to the side. As that thought goes, so do the feelings and behaviors that follow. That which you focus on expands. Focusing on the negative is essentially like fertilizing the weeds in your yard.

> That which you focus on expands.
> Focusing on the negative is essentially
> like fertilizing the weeds in your yard.

It's actually the flip side of channel capacity on full display. You're focused intently on one thing, and your mind is using all of its horsepower on that one thing. In essence, what you're focusing on grows larger.

So, if you think mostly about your problems, and place all of your mental focus on them, you're growing them larger in mental terms. They soon are occupying much more mental and emotional space than they normally would or should. That's when you start to lose perspective and run the risk of making decisions out of fear or even panic. It's the equivalent of trying to win a football game without ever putting your offense on the field.

What *does* enhance self-image? Learning to talk to yourself about what you do well and how you want to improve. Concentrating on solutions instead of problems, and bolstering that focus on the positive with self-talk and visualizations. In the words of Dr. Don Miguel Ruiz, bestselling author of the book *The Four*

Agreements, "the human mind is like fertile ground where seeds are continually being planted." Whatever seeds you plant in your mind are the ones that will grow—so use this knowledge to plant seeds for the things you want to achieve.[2]

> **What *does* enhance self-image? Learning to talk to yourself about what you do well and how you want to improve.**

Think about the last time you ran into a particularly thorny problem at work—something you worked on that was in the middle of not turning out the way you hoped. How did you talk to yourself before, during, and after that situation?

Is self-talk something you've ever consciously considered?

As we've been saying, the mind is more powerful than most people even comprehend. It would be a tragedy to waste that power by literally polluting it with negative and self-limiting thinking.

BUILDING A MENTAL PICTURE

Visualization has become a kind of catchword in sports—something you hear many athletes talk about in their post-game interviews.

It certainly makes sense when you're talking about a complicated physical process, like hitting a golf ball or a fastball. The player gets a huge benefit by actually "pre-seeing" himself or herself going through the act of making the big shot or kicking the game-winning field goal, complete with the surrounding scene and the emotions that come with doing it successfully.

The act of visualizing the action before it happens gets the mind and body prepared to actually do it in real life when the time comes. It is priming the mental and physical pump. Players who visualize their game are calmer, better prepared, and much more likely to succeed in high-pressure situations.

> The act of visualizing the action before it happens gets the mind and body prepared to actually do it in real life when the time comes. It is priming the mental and physical pump.

Visualization is a technique that you can use to help yourself even if your job never takes you within fifty miles of a batter's box or a tee at a PGA Tour event. The act of pre-seeing the important events in your day-to-day life in an office or at home is just as valuable as it would be if you were doing it as a professional athlete. The exact same principles hold true. By seeing yourself doing the things you'll soon have to do for real, you're getting your mind and body prepared early. There will be fewer emotional surprises when you get to the real event, and you will feel infinitely more prepared.

For example, Tom coaches a prominent Fortune 500 executive who received a big promotion at his firm. With that promotion came much more public responsibility—giving talks to shareholders and presentations to other large groups. The executive was terrific at the business of running a division and had a very strong technical background, but public speaking was something he had never enjoyed, and he really hadn't had to do it before as part of his work.

So Tom worked with him using the same process he had used with his basketball team years ago. They worked together to develop the executive's visualizing skill. First, they went through the next presentation the executive was scheduled to give. Tom asked him to imagine himself being introduced, and to focus on controlling his breathing. Then he imagined himself at the podium giving the beginning of the speech—not watching himself, but looking out at his audience, as if he were really there. In his mind he went through the main point of the presentation, still at the podium, and eventually visualized delivering the actual finish of the speech—how he was going to wrap it up.

The executive went through this process several times before the presentation, and when he walked up to the podium at the event itself, he felt like he was in familiar territory. He executed the steps just as he had been visualizing them over the past week— breathing during the introduction, nailing the opening, explaining the main point, and then sailing along to the finish.

THE MENTAL WORKOUT

As we said in the introduction, when Jason had one chance to convince the St. Louis Cardinals baseball team that he could bring value to the clubhouse, he picked the Mental Workout as the piece to share with the team in his ten-minute window. It's that important, and it can produce amazing results.

Jason designed the version we teach to world-class professional athletes and Olympians. It is designed to put them in an ideal mental state for competition and to integrate their mental performance with their physical training.

Most of us mere mortals don't have such a strong physical component in our day-to-day jobs, so the version we're going to teach you here was designed specifically for nonathletes, and is geared specifically toward mental performance and consistency in the business world. Done properly, it will take you about a hundred seconds to complete—which means that if you have time to brush your teeth, you have time to strengthen your mind. It has five basic steps:

1. Centering breath (breathe in for six seconds, hold for two, exhale for seven)
2. Identity statement (personally tailored positive self-talk)
3. Personal highlight reel (visualization of past and future success)
4. Identity statement (personally tailored positive self-talk)
5. Centering breath (breathe in for six seconds, hold for two, exhale for seven)

We'll go over each step in more detail below, and the steps are summarized again in the accompanying table. Your mind is a muscle just like your bicep. If you want your bicep to become stronger, you must complete bicep curls on a regular basis. The same is true for your mind. If you want to become mentally tough, you must complete *mental* workouts consistently.

Muscle deterioration begins within seventy-two hours of your last workout. Just as this is the case with your bicep, it also holds true for your brain. The goal should be to never let two days go by without some type of physical activity, nor should you go two days without completing a mental workout.

Step 1: Centering breath	Breathe in for six seconds, hold for two, breathe out for seven.
Step 2: Identity statement	Say a preconceived personal mantra to yourself that reflects your strength and desire for success.

Step 3: **Personal highlight reel**	Spend thirty seconds visualizing three "done-wells" from the previous twenty-four hours, and then spend another thirty seconds visualizing three things you want to do well in the upcoming twenty-four hours.
Step 4: **Identity statement**	Repeat your identity statement (same as Step 2).
Step 5: **Centering breath**	Take another centering breath to prepare yourself for the upcoming performance. Again, breathe in for six seconds, hold for two, breathe out for seven.

Centering Breath

To start your Mental Workout, you will give yourself some oxygen: breathe in for six seconds, hold that breath for two seconds, and then breathe out for seven seconds. When you modulate your breathing this way, you're controlling your state of arousal and corralling your body's natural response to stress.

The biological response to pressure is an elevated heart rate. Unfortunately, when your heart rate increases, your ability to think effectively decreases. A very powerful way to control heart rate is to do a centering breath. Breathing in for six seconds, holding for two seconds, and then exhaling for seven seconds gets air into your diaphragm and slows your heart rate, thus allowing your brain to operate optimally.

Identity Statement

Once you complete the breathing, recite your personal identity statement to yourself. Marathon runner Katie's is an awesome example: *Today I am strong. Today I am healthy. Today I am a beast.* You're free to use hers, or you can come up with one of your own—as long as it fits a few basic criteria. It needs to emphasize one of your positive qualities, and it has to pinpoint something you want to become.

The identity statement is a personal mantra that, when repeated over and over, will manifest itself into reality. Written in the present tense, an identity statement includes positive adjectives that describe the characteristics of the person you want to be and the level of success you want to achieve. When it comes to identity statements, let desire guide you. Don't worry as much about your current reality but, rather, focus on who you want to become. As the research on identity statements makes clear: the further from the truth, the more impactful.

Examples:

I am full of positive energy, I make $1 million per year, and I am an awesome mother and wife.

I outwork the competition every day, I am the most effective salesperson in the country, and I experience true love as a husband and a father.

Think it, see it, become it. I improve every day and I am consistently excellent as a leader, executive, and parent.

Repeating your identity statement in your Mental Workouts causes you to believe in yourself and in your ability to accomplish great things. It is a proactive approach to overcoming all the normal negative stuff that goes on in between a person's ears.

Personal Highlight Reel

Next, quietly visualize your own personal highlight reel for sixty seconds. See in your mind's eye three things you did well the previous day, and mentally rehearse the three most important things you need to do to in the upcoming twenty-four hours. In many ways, your mind works the same way a dominant Major League pitcher's does. He'll spend his sixty seconds visualizing himself hitting his exact spots with his slider and fastball, and following his first-inning game plan, while you'll picture things like giving a PowerPoint presentation at a sales meeting, or having a one-on-one with your supervisor that afternoon. The more specific you are in your visualization, the better. Just like the athlete, you are preparing yourself for success.

Visualizing is one of the most powerful tools in the field of performance psychology. It is safe to say that a person cannot perform at his or her potential without consistently using visualization as a pre-performance technique. To get the most out of visualizing, pay attention to the following three guidelines.

Guideline 1: Use the first-person vantage point. Visualizing from the first-person point of view means looking at the video through your own eyes, so you see the things you would actually see while performing the task or skill. If you know you have a sales meeting with a client over lunch, then visualize exactly what you will see, say, and feel while sitting in your lunch seat looking across the table at your client. Visualizing in this way will help make the mental image a three-dimensional experience that feels real enough to increase your confidence and skill most efficiently.

Guideline 2: Emotionally feel the way you want to feel. The video you play in your head needs to capture the emotional experience you want to have. Why? Because through visualization, you create your reality, and reality involves emotions. When you allow negative emotions, such as anger, embarrassment, or doubt, to creep into your performances, you will not deliver the performance you need to succeed. One way to banish these emotions is to consciously replace them with productive, positive emotions during visualization. The goal should be to feel and experience confidence in your visualizations.

Guideline 3: Visualize at the desired speed. Make sure to watch your mental clip in real speed—the speed you want your performance to be.

You may be wondering how you can visualize, for example, the delivery of an eighty-second script, a three-minute sales call, or a thirty-minute presentation at real speed if you have only a thirty-second block within your Mental Workout. That's a good question. You'll need to pick the most important specific moments within those events to run through in your visualization clips (for example, thinking through exactly what you will say in the first ten seconds of the presentation). Many people visualize in generalities, not knowing that it is far less effective than visualizing the details. The key is to visualize specific moments of success. Doing so allows for the success to actually generalize out to other areas that may not have been visualized. An NFL running back might see himself having a successful first run of the game, for example. Including detail and specifics when visualizing that very first run will set him up for increased success in each run thereafter as well.

Once you have a basic comfort level with visualization—and we mean just that, "comfort level," not expertise—you're ready to use one of the most powerful tools in your arsenal to improve your mental performance.

The rest of the Mental Workout is simple. After the highlight reel, once again repeat your identity statement. Then, bring yourself out of your focus-building concentration by completing another round of centered breathing—in for six seconds, hold for two, and out for seven.

Now, you're ready to focus and perform.

Plenty of our clients in the worlds of both sports and business have given us strange looks when we first introduced the Mental Workout as something they should try. All we can tell you is that the clients who have integrated it into their daily routine have seen huge benefits from it—something that shouldn't be so surprising.

After all, you wouldn't expect to build a lot of physical strength or endurance without training your body. Why would you expect to improve your mind without some kind of workout for it? Completing Mental Workouts develops the mental toughness necessary to control your self-talk. Having the strength between the ears allows you to replace negative thinking with thoughts that emphasize the positive.

We've been using this strategy with our clients for years, and there is no doubt, Mental Workouts will help you develop the mental toughness you see with high-level performers. You will train yourself to become the "go-to" player who makes the game-winning shot. When it comes to Mental Workouts, you can't afford not to try it.

The Big Why: What you think—or how you talk to yourself—dictates how you feel and behave, which in turn dictates if you will succeed or fail.

The Inversion Test: If you learn to talk to yourself in a positive way, you will find yourself consistently on the attack, thus speeding up the realization of success. If you continue speaking to yourself with negative tones, you will routinely play on the defensive—reducing your chances of success and increasing the time you spend stuck at the wall of underperformance.

Act Now: Take two minutes and attempt to complete one Mental Workout right now. Don't expect perfection or anything even close. Just try to work through the five steps.

Some examples of 100-second Mental Workouts from our clients:

PRO ATHLETE

Step 1—Centering breath (inhale for 6 seconds, hold for 2, exhale for 7, for 15 seconds total).

Step 2—Identity statement: I am more mentally and physically prepared than the competition. I am a *dominant* Major League pitcher (5 seconds).

Step 3—Personal highlight reel:

- Remembering 3 "done-wells" from the previous day (30 seconds total)

  Spent 5 minutes reading before bed (10 seconds)

  Made great nutrition choices at breakfast and lunch (10 seconds)

  Discussed concerns with Yadi (10 seconds)

- Imagining 3 "done-wells" in the upcoming day (30 seconds total)

  Spending 20 minutes in video room and identifying 1 weakness for each hitter I will face (10 seconds)

  Starting strong, staying strong, finishing strong in pre-game warm-up (10 seconds)

  Attacking mentality in first 3 pitches in the first inning (10 seconds)

Step 4—Identity statement: I am more mentally and physically prepared than the competition. I am a *dominant* Major League pitcher (5 seconds).

continues

Step 5—Centering breath (inhale for 6 seconds, hold for 2, exhale for 7, for 15 seconds total).

FINANCIAL ADVISOR

Step 1—Centering breath (inhale for 6 seconds, hold for 2, exhale for 7, for 15 seconds total).

Step 2—Identity statement: I am the happiest, healthiest, and best family man, friend, leader, and financial advisor in the world. I have a relentless solution focus and I always attack—no excuse (5 seconds).

Step 3—Personal highlight reel:

- Remembering 3 "done-wells" from the previous day (30 seconds total)

  Expressed my concerns to the Smiths about them not keeping enough emergency money in cash in their account (10 seconds)

  Completed my Success Log before leaving the office (10 seconds)

  Had great energy with Susan and the kids at home last night—played 2-inning game of kickball even though I was tired from the day (10 seconds)

- Imagining 3 "done-wells" in the upcoming day (30 seconds total)

  Calling high-net-worth client first and asking 4 feedback questions without getting defensive (10 seconds)

continues

> Seeing myself Organizing Tomorrow Today at precisely 3:00 p.m.—writing on paper "3 Most Important / 1 Must" (10 seconds)
>
> Leaving the office by 5:00 p.m. to be home by 5:20 (10 seconds)
>
> **Step 4**—Identity statement: I am the happiest, healthiest, and best family man, friend, leader, and financial advisor in the world. I have a relentless solution focus and I always attack—no excuse (5 seconds).
>
> **Step 5**—Centering breath (inhale for 6 seconds, hold for 2, exhale for 7, for 15 seconds total).
>
> ## SOFTWARE SALESMAN
>
> **Step 1**—Centering breath (inhale for 6 seconds, hold for 2, exhale for 7, for 15 seconds total.
>
> **Step 2**—Identity statement: I outwork the competition every day, and I am the most effective and precise presenter in the country (5 seconds).
>
> **Step 3**—Personal highlight reel:
>
> - Remembering 3 "done-wells" from the previous day (30 seconds total)
>
>   Was up by 5:00 a.m. and completed my workout by 5:45 (10 seconds)
>
>   Kept my focus in two client meetings and had excellent closes on both (10 seconds)

continues

Forced myself to go "lights out" by 9:00 p.m.
in preparation for the long day coming up
(10 seconds)

• Imagining 3 "done-wells" in the upcoming day
(30 seconds total)

Getting up by 5:00 a.m. and working out by 5:45
(10 seconds)

Starting strong, staying strong, finishing strong
on product call (10 seconds)

Step 4—Identity statement: I outwork the competition every day, and I am the most effective and precise presenter in the country (5 seconds).

Step 5—Centering breath (inhale for 6 seconds, hold for 2, exhale for 7, for 15 seconds total).

7

LEARN HOW TO
TALK WITH OTHERS

Steve Jobs was unquestionably one of the true business vision-aries of the modern age. He was the creative genius who cofounded Apple—and spearheaded the development of the mouse-controlled personal computer, the iPod, the iPhone, the iPad, and the iTunes music store. Known as the "father of the digital revolution," Jobs transformed the way people interact with technology on the most basic level. The powerful phone/computer/camera/jukebox you hold in your hand today is a direct result of his tireless work in product design and development and consumer marketing.[1]

For all of the work he did harnessing the design and technological advancements in Apple's products, Jobs's ultimate genius was in communicating exactly *why* a breakthrough product like the iPhone was something everyone both wanted and needed. He was able to get across both the technological superiority and the basic simplicity of Apple's devices in a way that avoided hyperbolic tech-speak. He explained how products like the iPod and iPhone would transform the average person's life in truly seamless ways.

Instead of intimidating customers with the prospect of having to learn how to use a complicated piece of hardware, Jobs communicated with them in a fundamentally different way. He explained—in language anybody could understand—how Apple's products could solve problems big and small. He introduced reasons to own an iPhone that hadn't even occurred to most of the people who ended up buying them.

Jobs did it in his highly anticipated annual presentations at Apple's new product launches. He walked around the stage casually in front of simple images on a large screen, speaking seemingly extemporaneously for forty-five minutes about the new products and how they fit into a user's life. He was famous for taking viewers down a simple path—introducing a big problem that hadn't been solved by the market, and then introducing the simple, elegant, impeccably designed solution.

But it wasn't a matter of a highly charismatic, natural speaker getting up and wowing the crowd in an off-the-cuff way, the way Bill Clinton notably does. Jobs was intensely private—and famously prickly in meetings with his team. He wasn't afraid to confront those who didn't live up to his standard. The natural, flowing presentations that launched so many iconic products were actually highly scripted, and they were the result of practice and repetition. The main objective was to make consumers wonder how they had ever lived without the latest iPhone or iPad.

To say his efforts were successful would be one of the biggest understatements of all time. When Jobs returned to Apple as CEO in 1996, the company was losing money and contemplating bankruptcy. In 2014, more than 200 million people were using iPhones, and Apple had a profit of $40 billion on sales of $182 billion—making it the most profitable publicly traded company in the world.

As Jobs would say about his exhaustive design sessions for the iPhone—preparation and communication makes the difference.

Jobs and Coach Wooden came from very different worlds, but on that point they would have agreed wholeheartedly. After Coach Wooden retired from UCLA in 1975, he spent most of his time close to his condo in Encino, California, attending games as a spectator and giving talks to different groups around Los Angeles. In 1989, Tom arranged for Coach Wooden to speak at the Edward Jones General Partners' Meeting. Before Coach's speech, the two got together, and they ended up talking basketball, as they often did. During the conversation about Wooden's famous high-post offense, Tom wanted to show that he could still handle the X's and O's like he did back in his own coaching days.

"I haven't coached for seven years, but I can still draw up that play," Tom said.

Coach Wooden nodded, and said he'd like to see it. Tom took a piece of paper from his briefcase and diagrammed the high-post offense. When he was done, Coach Wooden took the paper and looked it over carefully.

"How long did you say you had been out of coaching?" he asked.

"More than seven years," Tom said.

Wooden complimented him on his work, but then slid the paper back across the table. "That's really pretty good, but you left out one of the most important points," he said.

Tom was floored. He looked at the paper again and retraced his steps. He was convinced he had diagrammed all of the necessary movements. After a minute or two of not seeing the missing component, Tom slid the paper and pen back to Coach Wooden.

"You left out a very important detail. When the high post catches the ball, the guard must take two steps toward the goal to set up the play," said Wooden, adding the mark to the paper. "Tom, little details make big differences."

In that moment, it became even clearer to Tom how dynasties are created—by communicating the details.

Fifteen years after he had coached his last game, Wooden was still emphasizing the subtle detail of the guard's two-step cut—something that even the dozens of college and professional teams running his influential offense to this day haven't grasped.

Watch virtually any NCAA game today, and you'll see Wooden's high-post offense being run, but you won't see the guard make that critical movement to sell it to the defense.

To consistently win at the highest level, you have to be able to communicate effectively, with details.

———

What does the high-post offense have to do with communication skills?

Everything.

Basketball plays are like a language. They comprise a common set of information the people in a group use to communicate with each other. When everybody knows the play, they can move in concert. The group of five playing together can do much more than five individuals can working alone.

Likewise, you can have the best, most useful information in the world, but if you can't share it effectively, what good is it? Apple's products could have been groundbreaking, but the company's fight in the marketplace would have been much harder if Jobs hadn't done such a masterful job of communicating them for the consumer at launch. It doesn't matter what kind of business you're in—sales, technology, administrative, creative—the ability to communicate with the people around you is a critical skill.

If you aren't a natural speaker or communicator, you've probably watched some of the speeches people like Dr. Martin Luther

King Jr. and Winston Churchill were able to give and thought to yourself, *They're doing something I couldn't possibly ever learn.* In this, you are mistaken. You might not be able to copy their natural charisma, but you can certainly develop many of the same skills.

Studies have repeatedly shown that a vast majority of the impact from a presentation comes from the style of delivery—not just the words themselves. If you can learn to project self-confidence, you can become a terrific speaker. You don't have to be "supernatural" to connect with a client or move a team of five (or fifty, or five hundred) into action. You merely need to learn how to be confident when you communicate. And believe it or not, it is actually much easier than you might think.

All you need to do is understand some communication basics. Most people who struggle to talk to a group or give a basic presentation have a very basic problem: they are terrified. And being terrified keeps them from being prepared. For that matter, not being prepared can make giving a presentation much scarier than it should have been. The fear of failure can then become a self-fulfilling prophecy. It's a vicious cycle, with fear, lack of preparation, and low confidence intensifying one another.

Whether you're talking to a group of a thousand or making your pitch to an audience of a single person, the idea of speaking in front of people can simply be nerve-wracking. Even if you have a handle on what you want to get across, the thought of potentially making a mistake or otherwise looking foolish can be almost paralyzing. But turning this vicious cycle around is essential. As we've said before, the things you focus on expand—both good and bad. So, if you focus on how frightened you are to get up in front of people, or you think about all the mistakes you could conceivably make, what do you think will happen to those thoughts and concerns?

In this chapter, we will show you how to be prepared—which then will cause you to *feel* prepared and ready for what you're going to face. The good news is that with these techniques, you can turn the vicious cycle into a virtuous one: you can banish the fears with preparation and practice, and all that preparation and practice will lead to success and greater confidence. And the same rules work whether you are doing a large group presentation or planning a one-on-one meeting.

Preparation comes in three easy steps:

1. Write it.
2. Slow it.
3. Triangle it.

What does that mean? We'll explain.

STEP 1. WRITE IT

When Tom joined American Funds—the third largest mutual fund management organization in the world—in 1999, he was required to do what all other employees delivering the American Funds message must do—attend a two-day speech class, where they gave dozens of presentations. Every presentation was videotaped and analyzed by communications consultants and other experts.

It was a grueling exercise, and the way most tried to "beat" the test was to use extremely detailed notes. They tried to fill every two-minute talk with as much information as possible. They figured, *There must be SOMETHING in there somebody could use. I'll just give it all to them.*

It's totally natural to not want to come off as if you don't know your subject—especially in a pressure situation. So the totally natural response is to talk more and talk faster. Which is exactly wrong. Unfortunately, the more you say, the less believable you often become.

> **Unfortunately, the more you say,
> the less believable you often become.**

Even people in jobs that require tons of talking and presentations usually don't get this part right. Mutual fund companies have representatives called "wholesalers" whose job it is to present the different fund products to investment advisors and explain the benefits and features of the particular funds. A high-level advisor can be managing tens of millions of dollars for clients, and he or she usually prefers to work within a set range of funds he or she knows extremely well.

So there's a lot of competition for that valuable real estate among the wholesalers. But when you watch some wholesalers having a conversation with an advisor, you'd think the wholesaler was getting paid by the word. They speak to clients every day, yet they continue to blanket each client with a machine-gun volley of words. Unfortunately, the more you say, the harder you are to understand—the harder you are to follow. Think about it: the longer you speak, the more you must begin commenting on the less important points of your presentation. Unfortunately, people have a tendency to remember what you say last.

It's worth repeating—the more you say, the less believable you often become.

We've hit on the concept of channel capacity enough times by now that you should know what we're going to say next: there's a limit to what people can process in one sitting, and a limit to what they can comprehend within a string of sentences.

The best presenters are literally ruthless in organizing what they will say. They identify only the most important information that needs to be communicated, and they get rid of everything else. How does that work? They write a script. It's only after you get your thoughts organized to the point where you can go through and delete the less important parts that you'll start to feel ready to communicate.

It can certainly feel overwhelming to sit down and script out an entire presentation. But it's so worth it. By scripting your presentation, you are preparing, and by preparing, you will be banishing the fears you have about presenting. By preparing your message, you are also ensuring that you are saying only the most pertinent things—the things you want the client to really focus on and hear. You will find that your clients will listen and respond so much better than when you were winging it.

Start by mapping out the first five minutes, and then attack what you have written with the delete button.

Don't think for a second it won't be hard. It's really tough, but deleting is one of the most important parts of communicating effectively. You need to follow the simple rule that each presentation should have only one main point and a maximum of three subpoints. Loading more information in than that is asking for trouble. By making this part of your presentation razor-sharp, you're getting your message across in the cleanest, most efficient way.

Once you've finished the first five minutes, transition to the closing five minutes. By *finalizing* your talk, you're providing the destination for the rest of the presentation. Everything you say will be designed as a lead-in to bringing it home this way. Again, be very liberal with your "delete" button.

We've all sat in on brutally long, muddled presentations that wander from point to point. Either the presenter had a laundry list of information that he or she needed to get through, or there was a set amount of time on the clock that he or she needed to fill. There is no quicker way to get people to check out than to start droning on in a presentation that doesn't seem to be building to a main point or conclusion.

To drill this home, start thinking to yourself, *What if I only had five minutes total to speak? What would I say? What about three minutes? One minute?*

Practice the one-minute version of your talk, and you'll know you're getting to the core of the material.

Once you have your first five minutes and last five minutes mapped out, it's time to fill in what goes between. Remember, your goal is to include only the most important information. The ever-popular TED talks shoot for succinct presentations that touch on only the most pertinent information. TED presenters are thought to be some of the greatest speakers on the planet.

Once you figure out what content you want to include, it's time to bring the presentation to life with stories. Anecdotes and stories are what the audience will most remember. Be sure your stories have details that connect the audience to your topic and also build your credibility. We try to follow the rule that there should be one story for each point or subpoint. When your stories are in, you are ready to move to the next step.

STEP 2. SLOW IT

Once you've produced your script, it's time to learn how to deliver it.

By far the most common mistake people make is to deliver presentations too fast. It is important to remember that you've been thinking about what you plan to say for a long time—and, presumably, you're an expert on it. But everyone else isn't as far down the road as you are. This will likely be the first time they hear a lot of what you are trying to tell them, and they need time to digest it as you proceed.

Pace is the biggest indicator of confidence, and the best way to slow your pace is to purposefully use pauses. Every pause serves as an inverse catalyst. Your pace will be slower after each pause you use. Hearing your pace quicken should be your mental cue to take another pause. Don't be afraid to take three-second, five-second, and even seven-second pauses in between bits of information. If you don't slow down and simply pause between your thoughts, much of what you are saying is going to be lost. And the more information you cram into the intermittent thirty-second bursts of attention that the average listener can offer, the bigger the chance the person won't retain *any* of what you're saying.

It isn't a race, and it isn't a contest to prove how much you know. You can do much more to show strength and confidence—and attract your audience's attention—by pausing than you can by actually speaking. And when you project that confidence outward, it's actually absorbed by the people receiving the message.

It's how the greatest speakers of all time have communicated with their audiences. The idea is to figure out what the goal really is for the meeting and to serve that goal in the cleanest, most efficient way possible.

Plenty of coaches at the most elite level have strategic genius. But the best game plan in the world doesn't work if the players either can't follow what you're saying or have tuned you out.

One client of ours had been an extremely successful Olympic coach for several individual athletes, and had been hired by a large university to run its program in that sport. The coach was extremely knowledgeable, but had never worked either in an academic setting or with scholarship athletes in a team setting.

When the team assembled for the first time in training before the next season, the new coach handed all the players giant notebooks detailing every aspect of their training, along with a complete schedule for everything they needed to do every day until the first game of the season. During each practice, the coach would call players out and quiz them on the information in the book—and embarrass them if they stumbled on the answer.

There's no question that a few of the highest-achieving members of the team thrived on the discipline and hard-core guidance they got from the new coach. But the rank-and-file team members quickly got lost, and the overall team results weren't what the new coach—or the administration—expected.

Our goal was to help the coach preserve the quality of the guidance he was giving to the players, but to manage the stream of information so that the players were accountable for what they needed to know, but reassured by the basic fairness of the level of expectation. The first step was to "delete" almost 70 percent of the original team notebook. The second step was to help the coach learn to communicate at a slow enough pace—one fundamental idea per day, often covering the same fundamental day after day to ensure full understanding. Over time, that translated into a set of core, nonnegotiable principles that became the repeated focus of every practice.

Most speakers and coaches are afraid of repetition, but the best communicators have learned to *use* repetition.

> Most speakers and coaches are afraid
> of repetition, but the best communicators
> have learned to *use* repetition.

Dozens of studies have shown that when you're trying to give people information that you want them to retain, offering more than two or three discrete things is a huge mistake. This basic human reality drives how we schedule every single seminar we do. We take people through one or two facets of training, offer some guidance in real-world scenarios, then break and give the attendees a chance to digest and practice the information before we move on to the next phase.

You can't expect to offer people half a dozen pieces of information and expect them to somehow synthesize it on the spot and make a well-informed decision about it. In fact, if you *do* put your colleagues, clients, and potential clients in that position repeatedly, you're going to find you have far fewer of all three over time. Slow down and you will find yourself a whole lot more on target with your audience.

In addition, you will find that slowing down is actually much easier for you as a speaker. You will be able to think about what you are saying as you are saying it. Doing so will make it much easier to follow your script and maintain your confidence.

STEP 3. TRIANGLE IT

The whole goal of presenting in a group, either with clients or in your office setting with colleagues, is to deliver your message in a way that gets the receiver to take action.

A basketball team runs its offense through a set of plays. When those plays get added to the playbook, how do you think the players on the team learn both the plays and how to move together on the floor? Does the coach hand out the playbook, explain the play one time, and hope for the best when game time comes? Or does the coach break down the play into components and explain each player's part, and then supervise as the players repeat the play again and again in practice, so that it becomes second nature?

The answer is obvious in a basketball setting. Why does it seem so much less obvious in the business world?

A very effective method for practicing communication is something called the "success triangle": for the three days before your big presentation or meeting, spend three separate three-minute segments per day mentally rehearsing what you want to say and how you want to say it. We advise people to ritualize the triangle training by spending the three minutes each day just prior to each meal—breakfast, lunch, and dinner.

If you have more time than three days before, by all means expand the practice into as many days as you can. But look at the success triangle and the three-day window as the ideal minimum requirements. If for some reason you have less time than that— maybe you've been called on to fill in tomorrow unexpectedly— don't sweat it. You can still get most of the benefit of preparation. Get in as many of the three-minute segments as you can, but be sure to give yourself at least sixty minutes of break time in between.

A personal injury attorney client of ours was terrified about an upcoming case. Although our client was very competent and quite prepared, it was her first time presenting a case in front of a jury. For three days before the trial opened, she spent three minutes three times a day visualizing herself in the courtroom with the judge and jury, slowly going through the first minute of her opening argument word by word.

When the trial started, the attorney was actually surprised by her confidence level and the smoothness with which she presented. Her client eventually won the ruling, and the attorney so impressed her supervisors that she got on the fast track to become only the second female partner in the firm.

This triangle technique is the same one that professional athletes use to visualize how they will perform in an event. You're just using it in a different setting. When you visualize the actual situation you'll be in, and rehearse the exact words you're going to say—and how you want to feel when you're doing it—you're preparing yourself for game day. You'll be ready for any surprises.

It's important to point out that there's a big difference between "practicing" and mentally rehearsing with the success triangle. Practice *can* be useful, but not necessarily as effective as mentally rehearsing. If you're trying to develop a skill you don't have—like learning how to hit a golf ball—structured practice at a driving range is going to help you. But if you're a good player, basic practice is often little more than exercise. You're not simulating game conditions, or putting yourself in the same frame of mind you will be in when it's time to compete.

Anybody can hit it long and straight on the practice tee, when you have an unlimited bucket of balls next to you and there's no penalty for missing. Mentally rehearsing with the success triangle is different: it puts you right there, in the situation. You're "pre-creating" the pressure of game day, so you can feel it, experience it, and be prepared for it.

> Mentally rehearsing with the success triangle is different.
> You're "pre-creating" the pressure of game day,
> so you can feel it, experience it, and be prepared for it.

The research is overwhelming. Using a technique like the success triangle is at least seven times more effective than rote practice alone. In other words, visualizing a presentation, using the triangle, for nine minutes per day is the equivalent of standing in front of the mirror for an hour and reciting it word for word. It works, and it saves you time.

GOING ONE ON ONE

You might be reading this and thinking to yourself, "It's great to know, but in my role, I don't do much speaking in front of other people." Regardless of how much "public speaking" you're doing, you still have to interact with people on a one-to-one basis in the business world. The skills we're taking about help build confidence, and confidence is the single most important ingredient for communication success, whether you're talking to a group of 150 people or 1 person across the table from you in a sales meeting.

Affirmations and positive thinking are great, and your confidence is going to really grow when you start using the concrete tools of preparation to sharpen the points you want to make. All of the same principles we've been talking about when it comes to "public" speaking still apply, but when you're in a closer setting, such as a one-on-one meeting or a small group, a few more factors come into play. You need to be able to stay calm, listen, and control the energy level in your voice.

Let's take those one at a time.

When it's just you and another person on a call, or you're sitting two feet from somebody and you're trying to get and keep that person's undivided attention, you have to be tuned in to a finer level of detail than when you are doing a presentation to a larger group.

In a presentation, you're controlling the show from start to finish, and repetition and preparation are your friend. You know the route you're going to take, and the words will be familiar territory. In a conversation, that's still true to a certain extent—you need to know your stuff—but you're also responding to what the other person will say. It's like tennis. You can have a good scouting report and know what the other person's game is like, but you still have to run down each shot and return it.

Because you're interacting back and forth, you need to be as tuned in to what's coming from the other person as you are comfortable with what you're delivering. To do that, you need to be able to stay calm. If you have a high-stakes conversation on your plate, you simply aren't going to perform as well if the running thought through your mind, as it's happening, is, "Just don't screw this up."

It isn't any different from learning to perform a physical task under competitive pressure, like athletes do. The single best method of staying calm is to control your breathing by using the centering breath we have already talked about. In the sixty seconds before the beginning of a presentation or meeting, be sure to take at least one centering breath (inhale for six seconds, hold for two, exhale for seven). While the other person is talking during the conversation, find times to take additional centering breaths. You don't need to announce what you're doing, and believe it or not, your deep breathing will be undetected by your counterparts.

It might sound strange to talk about a relaxation technique like breathing when it comes to a conversation, but it really works, and it's an extremely valuable tool to know. Not only does it help you get your heart rate under control, but it allows you to become a much more effective listener. It redirects nervous energy into a more positive, productive place.

Any salesman with a few months of experience on the same job can recite the benefits of a given product off the top of his or her head. *Knowing* the information isn't the separating factor by itself. It's *knowing* the information that way, but also having the ability to deliver the information in a manner that causes the other person in the conversation to take notice and to interact. The fact is, you're doing more to establish a true *conversation* when you slow down your end of it. Roughly 20 percent of communicating is speaking, while 65 percent is listening. Yet, when it comes to communication, a vast majority of instruction is aimed at how to speak more effectively. Rarely are you prompted to learn to listen better. Most of us fall into this common communication trap at one time or another. We get so caught up in planning what we're going to say next that we don't pay full attention to what the other person is actually saying.

This situation will often lead to a choppy series of interruptions, where each person thinks what he or she has to say is more important than what the other is saying. If you are interrupting someone, there is no possible way you are truly listening. Interrupting sends the distinct message that you really only care about what you are saying. The opportunity for listening and learning is getting lost. By slowing down, you also allow yourself to be a better listener. You have more time to think about what you're saying, more time to say it correctly, and more time to listen to what the other person is saying.

Your voice is also an important tool when you're in a one-on-one situation. When presenting to a large group, you have the advantage of practice—and maybe even a microphone. You can get your message crafted and practice delivering it at the right speed with the right voice energy. When it's a more intimate setting, you're balancing getting your message across with being responsive to the other person. That causes many people to start to speed up. They talk faster and faster—or louder or softer—and by the end of the conversation, the voice energy they hoped for wasn't there.

You can improve your presentation by consciously evaluating your voice and the speed of your delivery. Instead of trying to set the record for the amount of material covered in one call or conversation, change your approach to value calmness, positive energy in your voice, and the act of leaving conversational room for the other person to evaluate each thing you're saying.

If you're a fast-paced person—and even if you're more of a medium-paced talker—it will definitely feel strange at first to slow down. But you will start to notice some amazing things when you do. The person on the other side of the conversation will begin to subconsciously attribute more authority to you and more weight to what you're saying. When you both present meaningful content and leave openings for thoughtful responses, you're putting yourself in special company.

Maybe you work from an office and have little face-to-face contact with outside clients. Even if so, you're not off the hook, because the rules still apply to other kinds of communication. Think about the conversations you have over the phone. We realize that phone calls are becoming more and more scarce, thanks to the advent of text messaging. But personal connections still need to be made. And most people spend their half of the phone conversation waiting for the other person to stop talking so they can announce what they want to say. In addition, communication gets even more jumbled in a phone conversation than in face-to-face interactions, because on the phone you can't see the other person and react to his or her body language.

The advice is the same for phone conversations as for other kinds of communication: when you're on the phone, slow down at least 20 percent more than you think you need to. Leave some air between your sentences. Let the person on the other end catch up with you. Whether you're giving a presentation to a hundred people in a conference room, talking to a potential client on the phone, or having a meeting with three colleagues across the table, you have to accept that channel capacity is going to prevent you from cramming those other people full of information. You must slow down to be effective.

Here's a very simple example that illustrates that point. A financial advisor who had been through several of our training programs called looking for some advice. He had a conversation scheduled for the next day with a client who had $10 million to invest—a potential account that would have tremendously impacted his bottom line for the year. It was the biggest potential client he had ever had the chance to meet, and he was feeling very nervous.

"What do I say?" he asked us. "This guy could potentially hand me a check for $10 million. How do I open? What do I bring to this meeting?"

We started with the basics of scripting out the two main reasons he was the best man for the job and then moved on to practicing it. He focused on of how to control breathing and heart rate, so that his nervousness wasn't written all over his face—or his voice. Then, we talked about ways to inspire the potential client to engage in the conversation, instead of just listening to a prepared "speech."

After a minute or two of small talk to open the conversation, the advisor said to the potential client, "I know your time is valuable, and there are some questions I need to ask you." He then paused for a few seconds. "But before I ask them, I want to assure you that anything we talk about will remain strictly confidential." He then moved on to his two main points and closed with a very strong request for the prospect's business.

It might not seem like a big thing, but the advisor said that the moment he stressed confidentiality, the potential client and his attorney both relaxed and sat back in their chairs. As soon as the advisor saw them relax this way, his confidence level soared. He knew they had engaged in the discussion, and he let his preparation and knowledge take over from there.

He earned the business.

The Big Why: In the business world, a person's skill level is largely realized based on his or her ability to communicate in a confident, efficient manner.

The Inversion Test: Great communicators will experience great success. Poor communicators will experience great failure.

Act Now: Write on paper the first minute, word for word, of what you will say in the next presentation you will deliver.

Some examples from our clients:

PRO ATHLETE

(pitcher talking to his catcher before playing an upcoming opponent that the team has historically had trouble with)

The first thing I would like to say is, thank you. I don't think I tell you enough how much I appreciate all the work you put into making me look good. I know your job is somewhat thankless, but I want to be at least one person who thanks you often for your preparation and approach (three-second pause). Let's figure out how to finally beat these guys. I want your input. What is the one thing you most think I need to be focused on if we are going to be lights-out tomorrow night?

FINANCIAL ADVISOR

(coffee meeting with a prospective client)

Good to see you Jim. Last week when I met with Tom and Susan they both had great things to say about you. I know you're busy, so with your permission, I'd like to skip the small talk and get to the heart of the matter. With that said, let me ask you a question, if I may (three-second pause). What is the single biggest thing you are hoping I can help with?

(This is where it becomes very important to listen. The thrust of the conversation from here forward must be centered on meeting Jim's one biggest need.)

---

continues

PHYSICIAN

(speaking to a group of twenty to twenty-five attorneys, with the goal of having them give him referral business and using him as an expert witness in medical litigation)

Let me begin by asking all of you a question (three-second pause). If your mother or your father, or one of your children, was injured, and it was possible that the injury was life threatening, would you have extreme confidence in any one medical professional? Think about that for a second (three-second pause). I would like to cover with you, in the next fifteen minutes, the three reasons why, if, God forbid, a life-threatening injury did occur to a loved one, friend, or client, you should seriously consider thinking of me and my team as the resource for providing the highest level of care.

CRUNCH TIME

In a basketball game between two evenly matched teams, the outcome often isn't decided until the last two minutes of the game. The team that's behind plays with a little desperation and makes a run, and it's up to the team that's ahead to handle the surge. Crunch time, when the game is close, is what defines champions—the teams and players we remember long after they're done playing.

In terms of this book, we're now in crunch time. The coach has called a time out. There's two minutes to play—and one chapter to go. The goal is to take what you've learned since halftime and integrate it into an end-game plan.

Before you move on to the last chapter, "Become Abnormal," go through the same process with the main discussion points of these three chapters that you did with Chapters 1 to 4. Pick the one main point that resonates with you (or choose one of your own), and pass it along as a teacher to one of your friends, relatives, or colleagues. Remember, when you teach it, you learn it.

CHAPTER 5: EVALUATE CORRECTLY

1. Learn to recognize the done-wells. People have a biological tendency to dwell on the things that aren't going well and that which you focus on expands.

2. Focusing on your level of effort, on your commitment to a process, and on what you're doing well overall is far more effective than evaluating yourself through the perfectionist lens.
3. Learn to give yourself mini-evaluations throughout the day. Status reports like this will give you time and information to make necessary adjustments.
4. _____
_____

CHAPTER 6:
LEARN HOW TO TALK TO YOURSELF

1. Become more aware of how you talk to yourself—the goal is "no more negative self-talk."
2. Completing the Mental Workout regularly builds mental toughness—and thought control. This will give you the mental toughness needed to become much more positive and much less negative.
3. When you visualize, you prepare your mind and body for positive growth and action.
4. _____
_____

CHAPTER 7:
LEARN HOW TO TALK WITH OTHERS

1. Know your material by writing a script.
2. Slow down and breathe.
3. Nail the presentation by spending three separate three-minute practice sessions per day in the three days leading up to your event (the success triangle).

4. _____

_____

Coach Wooden and Charlie Munger have been two of the most influential thought leaders in our professional lives, and they both emphasized many of the same basic philosophies. One of their core values was the idea that nobody—no matter how much they had achieved—should stop learning.

When you embrace the idea that you should always be learning, you're deciding to live a life open to information and experiences. You're not only giving yourself the chance to reach your own full potential, but also fully engaging in the world and the people around you.

Think about it. When you're on a team or in a group, and one of the other people doesn't want to hear any of the information you want to share, what is your inclination toward that person? We all respond much better to people who are open to hearing and learning. That works both ways.

As you go through the process of teaching one of these key points to somebody else, don't hesitate to make some notes here or on any other page. Coach Wooden devoured books on many subjects during the off-season, always looking for information that could help him coach and mentor his players. And you could always tell which books were his, because he filled the margins with notes and reminders.

It's a great habit to get into.

8

BECOME ABNORMAL

"Normal." That's a word that often signifies a quality a person is striving to achieve. How many times have you heard somebody say, "I just want to live a normal life"? Or, "I can't wait until things get back to normal"?

Normal is fine. Acceptable. Average. But if you want to do great things, you need to be *abnormal*.

We've covered many of the tools that can be used to take your success to the next level. But we would be ripping you off if we didn't talk about the real challenges that come when you try to make these kinds of changes.

Many people can sleepwalk through their professional and personal lives and reach a sort of equilibrium. They do enough to get by where they are, but nothing more. They aren't really doing anything wrong enough to make headlines, but they aren't moving up, either.

You would not have made it this far into this book if you were one of those people. And we would be ripping you off if we let *normal* be the aspiration you took away from these lessons. As the title of this chapter says, the goal is to be . . . *abnormal*.

It can be tempting—and it's becoming easier than ever with all our distractions—to push things off into the future, or to give yourself blanket forgiveness every time you slide on a goal or a commitment and there's a "reasonable" excuse.

Maybe you want to break an earnings goal at your company, but you haven't gotten around to taking the certification classes you need to get there. There'll be more time in the spring, right? (Or the summer, or the fall . . .) You definitely want to lose that extra fifteen pounds you've been carrying. And once you finish this one big project, you're going to commit the time to do it, right? And if not then, then right after the kids leave for summer camp. Then the time will be right.

We hate to say it, but the time is never *perfectly* right. If you're waiting for the perfect moment and perfect information so you can make the perfect decision, you're going to wait forever. The truth is, life is a bumpy road. You're going to have periods of smooth sailing, and times when you're faced with adversity and stress. To be *abnormal*, you need the ability to accept the adversity and stress that is inevitably coming your way—and not only survive it, but thrive on it. That happens when you have confidence in the tools at your disposal—the concepts we've been talking about—and when you're familiar with the test.

The test preparation business offers a great analogy. In the test-prep world, the first order of business for any instructor is to get the student familiar with the test format. When you walk into the classroom and are handed the test booklet, your level of anxiety is greatly reduced if you know, in general, what kinds of questions are coming, and how long you have to complete each section. Just by eliminating the fear of the unknown—and establishing a frame of reference for what's coming—you've allowed yourself to concentrate on the actual task at hand instead of trying to corral your emotions.

Of course, knowing the format is only part of the battle. If you don't know any of the material, you're still going to struggle. But a combination of knowing the material—or, in terms of this book, mastering one or more of the concepts we've been discussing—and being ready for the test itself is a powerful position to be in.

You know the material. Now, we want to warn you about three of the performance "viruses" that could cause you the most trouble in your quest for abnormal. We call them the "The Trap of the Viable Excuse," "Focusing on What You Can't Control," and "Giving In to Problem-Centric Thought."

Just knowing what these viruses are—and how they hide in plain sight in your everyday life—will help you establish immunity to them before they have a chance to establish themselves. And if you do start to see symptoms, you'll be able to stay calm, keep your perspective, and apply an effective antidote.

VIRUS #1:
THE TRAP OF THE VIABLE EXCUSE

In Major League Baseball, nothing spreads faster than a scouting report.

Once the "book" on a player has been established, news travels. If a guy murders inside fastballs—or can't hit a curveball—it doesn't take long for everybody in the league to know. Once everybody knows what a player can (and can't) do, it's up to the player to make whatever adjustments need to be made.

Jason had been working with one of his baseball clients for about a year and a half when the player ran into what we call the "Trap of the Viable Excuse." The player was a veteran with a lot of success under his belt, but he went through a season in which his batting average dropped by more than 50 points.

The word had gotten out that the player was struggling to hit breaking balls. Of course, almost immediately, all he started seeing in each at-bat was breaking balls. His weakness had been exposed, and now it was getting attacked. Every time Jason brought up the obvious subject of learning to improve how he responded to breaking balls, the player had the same response.

He said that he had never been a good breaking ball hitter—not in high school, college, or the pros—but he destroyed fastballs. That's what he was paid to do, and that's what he did. For one season, he clung to that idea, but the results got even worse.

After the season, Jason once again brought up the touchy subject of addressing the problem. The player started in on his speech about never being a good breaking ball hitter, but before he got to the second sentence, Jason respectfully stopped him. "I know you're a professional hitter, and I know you get paid to hit fastballs," Jason said. "But nobody is throwing you fastballs anymore, and if we don't figure this breaking ball thing out, we're both going to get fired."

At first, the player was angry about getting confronted that way. To ease the tension, Jason explained that what the player was experiencing was very common. He had fallen into the "Trap of the Viable Excuse."

Viable excuses are so hard to overcome because they sound so reasonable. They're disguised to the point that the person doesn't even realize they're using an excuse.

> Viable excuses are so hard to overcome because they sound so reasonable. They're disguised to the point that the person doesn't even realize they're using an excuse.

Here's the most dangerous part. The more "reasonable" the excuse is, the more you're willing to accept the failure and make it your new normal.

> The more "reasonable" the excuse is,
> the more you're willing to accept the failure
> and make it your new normal.

That's the "Trap of the Viable Excuse." When you accept it, you're accepting a permanent lowering of your personal standards.

Many, many clients have told us some variation of this line: "I'm not making any excuses, but let me tell you why I couldn't get the work done that we talked about last time. . . . " The reason could be anything—traffic, bad weather, not feeling your best, or any of the other real issues that pop up in real life. Viable excuses all contain a significant element of truth. Of course there will be obstacles that appear in your path toward success. Highly successful people have learned that even when obstacles present themselves, they still have an obligation to find a way to get it done.

> Highly successful people have learned that even
> when obstacles present themselves, they still
> have an obligation to find a way to get it done.

But the only right answer—if you're truly committed to improvement—is to learn how to be completely accountable for what you do, even in the face of adversity. That means no excuses. Not even viable ones.

When a person makes an excuse, it serves as a pacifier to the mind. The excuse itself gets the attention, rather than the reality that a commitment was not honored. Shifting the mental focus to the excuse stalls progress. Avoiding excuses allows a person to experience strong negative emotions—and those negative emotions can serve as the internal motivation needed for growth and improvement.

Developing a "no-excuse" mentality can often make you become "abnormal" in the best way. People who don't make excuses are the ones you want on your team. They are the ones you can count on when the pressure mounts. They are the all-stars, the leaders, the consistent winners in life.

> People who don't make excuses are the ones you want on your team. They are the ones you can count on when the pressure mounts. They are the all-stars, the leaders, the consistent winners in life.

We're not talking about making terrible choices here. There *are* circumstances when getting something done isn't the priority. If you're choosing being at a business meeting over being with a family member who is having a medical emergency, you're not making good choices. You do want to "defer to intelligence," and that means making those logical calls when needed.

When you accept accountability, you're creating a powerful internal dynamic. Instead of being externally motivated by what is happening around you, you're becoming internally motivated.

> When you accept accountability, you're creating a powerful internal dynamic. Instead of being externally motivated by what is happening around you, you're becoming internally motivated.

Jason's client quickly started coming up with ways he could improve how he handled breaking balls. He resolved to take twenty pitches from the mechanical pitching machine every day—half with no bat, just to improve his pitch recognition. His ability to find solutions almost immediately increased once he stopped making the excuse. By the end of the season, the player had doubled his success against breaking pitches, and his overall batting average was back where it had been two years before.

You probably don't have to think too hard to remember some common viable excuses from your own life. Do any of these sound familiar?

- There's no way I can get to that. I'm too busy.
- I'm doing my part, but the rest of the team is screwing up.
- How can I do what I'm supposed to do? Our technology is so out of date.
- I was exhausted.
- I didn't get the breaks that other person got.

It certainly feels better in the moment to come up with a "viable excuse" about why something didn't happen successfully. But, as we said, it lowers the bar. And it also prevents you from taking advantage of one of the most powerful change motivators there is: negative emotion. Fear. Disgust. Disappointment. Anger. People do everything they can to avoid feeling those emotions. But the most successful people approach it a different way: they take those negative emotions and *use* them as a fuel for improvement.

When you use a viable excuse, you're stopping yourself from feeling bad enough that you want to make the change that will prevent you from coming up short the next time. The excuse makes it okay to underperform in the moment—and, most importantly and unfortunately, in the future as well. Operating with a true "no excuses" mentality certainly takes some guts, and you'll probably be apologizing much more than you're used to. But just the act of setting the bar higher for yourself will improve your performance, and it will remind you that you're the one in control of your thoughts, goals, and actions.

VIRUS #2: FOCUSING ON
WHAT YOU CAN'T CONTROL

It's early 2009, and the stock market is in the free-fall that would see it drop more than 50 percent from its high in October 2007.[1]

Tom was working with American Funds, and he traveled to different offices around the country to take the pulse of advisors and try to give them some guidance on how to help clients who had seen their portfolios crushed by the downturn. As Tom made what he called his "world tour," he knew he needed to offer a straightforward strategy that would help advisors—and clients— fend off panic and make rational decisions with the right amount of perspective.

It started with two lists. First, Tom asked the advisors to make a list of the things they could control.

Effort.
Knowledge.
Organization.
Attitude with clients.
Tone of voice.
Frequency of communication.

You get the idea.

Then, Tom asked them to make a list of the things they *could not* control.

The markets.

The news.
The presidential election.
What other advisors were saying or doing.
Commodity prices.
Natural disasters.

When the lists were finished, Tom asked the advisors which list they had been spending most of their time thinking (and worrying) about. Virtually everyone—ninety-five out of one hundred—said they had been spending most of their time in crisis mode worrying about the things on the second list.

At that point in the presentation, Tom stopped and told each advisor to get on the phone and just concentrate on *one* thing they could control—his or her tone of voice. By taking control of one thing that was available to *be* controlled, the advisors felt the ground under their feet. Then, they could move on to some of the other items on the list and build out from there. Instead of starting the day on defense, dreading the conversations that were going to come, they resolved to come into the day with a plan of attack and start on offense.

Tom's advice wasn't new. He adapted it from a lesson he had learned from Coach Wooden. Early in Wooden's career at UCLA, the basketball team practiced in a building called the B.O. Barn (named after the distinctive "smell"). They had to share space with the wrestling and gymnastics teams, and many times, all three teams had to practice at the same time.

Driving home one night, Wooden was concerned because the players had been distracted by some commotion from the other teams during practice. But as he continued his drive, he realized that he was spending a lot of energy getting upset about something that was out of his control. He decided right then that he was only going to focus his energy on the factors he *could* control.

He later said that decision was the fuel that took his coaching to the next level. People think that Wooden was an instant success at UCLA, but he lost the first four games he coached in the NCAA Tournament. Focusing on what they could control, the Bruins would go on to win ten national championships in a twelve-year period. The success of the 1964 team—which went 30–0 and packed the 1,300-seat Barn—led the school to build Pauley Pavilion, a bigger, better-smelling, and less distracting arena.

The lesson Coach Wooden learned—and passed on to Tom in his own handwriting—is that focusing on the things you can't control actually hurts your ability to focus on the things you *can* control. This is the way Coach Wooden said it:

> 4-17-03
> Dear Tom,
> Concern yourself with what you can control.
>   If you get too caught up, concerned, engrossed or involved over the things over which you have no control, it will have an adverse effect on the things over which you have control.
> Love,
> John

It goes beyond the time suck that automatically comes with spinning your wheels dwelling on something that won't change—no matter how much time you actually spend thinking about it. The bigger problem is how it impacts your ability to prioritize—and how it steals your time, energy, and creativity.

People spend so much time thinking about things on the "Can't Control" side because, frankly, it's easier. If you're angry about something that Congress did or fuming about the weather, you don't actually have to come up with a plan of action, and there's ultimately no accountability. The "Can't Control" virus is extremely contagious, and it's one that can take hold of you multiple times a day. Luckily, awareness is the best defense against it. The key is to learn to recognize when you are allowing yourself to focus on things you cannot control. Typically, frustration is the alarm that lets you know you're emphasizing things out of your control. When you feel frustrated, it is often a response to your thoughts being centered outside of your control.

Your strategy should be the same one Tom used at the meetings during his world tour. Make a simple two-column chart on a piece of paper and write down a list of a few things you can control. Then move over to the other side and make the same kind of list of things you can't.

Common examples of things you cannot control:

- Competing in a hostile environment
- Bad officials
- The media
- Other people
- The weather

Common examples of things you can control:

- Activity
- Preparation
- Organization
- Attitude
- Effort

Then ask yourself, "Which side have I been spending most of my time on?"

Frustration is the direct result of the "Can't Control" virus. It may sound overly simplistic, but anytime you feel frustrated, pull out a piece of paper and create your own "Can and Cannot" control chart. Doing so will help jump-start you into action toward those things you can control in life. It might even be helpful to highlight one of the most common "Can't Control" viable excuses you tend to use, to sort of warn yourself in advance to be ready to fight it off!

> Anytime you feel frustrated, pull out a piece of paper and create your own "Can and Cannot" control chart. Doing so will help jump-start you into action toward those things you can control in life.

VIRUS #3: GIVING IN TO PROBLEM-CENTRIC THOUGHT

In Game Six of the 2011 World Series, the St. Louis Cardinals were trailing by three runs as late into the game as it's possible to go without it being over—with one strike left in the bottom of the ninth inning. But even as Cardinals fans were preparing for the Texas Rangers to clinch the title, the Cardinals players refused to give in to what was seemingly inevitable.[2]

Instead of concentrating on the negatives of the moment and the problem at hand, the players forced themselves to think about solutions. Refusing to focus on the scoreboard, the pressure, or how close to defeat they were, they channeled their thoughts toward the fundamental details of having a "good at-bat." They kept to the routine that had gotten them to the World Series in the first place—waiting for good pitches to hit, not trying to do too much in an at-bat.

Player after player showed he thrived on the biggest stage. David Freese laced a triple off the wall, scoring three runs and sending the game to extra innings. Once again, the Rangers took the lead on a two-run homer by Josh Hamilton. This time, Lance Berkman was the last-strike hero for the Cardinals, tying the game again with an RBI single. In the eleventh inning, Freese would strike again, this time hitting the game-winning home run that would send the series to a Game Seven—and ultimately a World Championship for the Cardinals.

It was the first time in World Series history that a team came back from two different two-run deficits in the ninth inning or later in the same game. Freese's homer was only the fourth walk-off in World Series history, and the Cardinals became the first team in Series history to score in the eighth, ninth, tenth, and eleventh innings.

After the game, the players talked about how they refused to let their thoughts become poisoned by thinking about the possibility of a negative outcome: they thought about what they had done well up to that point in the game and what needed to happen to succeed, and that gave them confidence that they could continue.

That makes the St. Louis Cardinals abnormal. Most "normal" people would fall back to the "default." In this case, the default is what we call "problem-centric thinking," a concept we've discussed earlier in this book. If you're confronted with a problem—anything from a simple flat tire to a complex medical issue—your first reaction is probably going to be to obsess about the problem itself. But if you occupy all of your time and energy thinking about the problem itself, it will cause that problem to grow larger in your mind. Remember what we established in Chapter 6—the concept that what you focus on expands.

It doesn't happen just in the mind, either. When you allow your mind to focus on a problem, your brain releases certain neurotransmitters that cause you to feel terrible physically, and those neurotransmitters also significantly hamper your creativity and intelligence. The more you focus on the problem, the more likely it is for you to look at the now-larger problem and start thinking about quitting. Focusing on problems has the potential to send you into a vicious negative cycle. For example, you might be a small business owner who gets most of his or her business from one huge client. That client goes through financial problems and eliminates your contract with no warning. You could get angry, wipe everything off your desk, and curse out your contact at that company—which would be quintessential problem-centric thinking.

The next natural emotion after that would be a feeling of despair or hopelessness:

How will I ever replace that business?
I might as well close the doors for good.
I knew I shouldn't have relied so heavily on that one client.

As we said with the viable excuse trap, we're not here to make any value judgment about the reasons behind what happened. It happened. Now what?

Strong, resilient people have what we call a "Relentless Solution Focus," or RSF. If a person with great RSF was in the same situation and lost that big client, he or she wouldn't be some kind of emotionless robot—the loss would sting. But the immediate, laser-sharp focus would be on finding the solution path, and doing it in less than sixty seconds.

We say "solution path" because many, many problems aren't solved with one lightning strike of an idea, obviously. A solution is a process, and there are steps to that process. In RSF, your goal when presented with a problem is to identify one step within sixty seconds that you can take that will make the situation better— even if only by a small increment of improvement. RSF is not about finding the "perfect" solution but, rather, about just identifying some kind of improvement. It's called the "+1 solution," because any improvement whatsoever to the current situation is part of a solution. The +1 concept has been credited numerous times with making the previously deemed impossible actually possible.

One important key is to transfer your thinking about the problem from worry to RSF within sixty seconds, to avoid those negative neurotransmitters from being released into your bloodstream. The great news is that when you direct your thoughts from problems to solutions, your brain releases a whole new set of neurotransmitters. The neurotransmitters on the solutions side actually work to make you feel better, and they significantly improve your creativity, intelligence, and memory. It's as if you have a powerful army in your head, and all it needs is the right orders.

When we focus on small, incremental improvements instead of perfection, the human spirit takes over, and all things become much more possible.

> When we focus on small, incremental improvements instead of perfection, the human spirit takes over, and all things become much more possible.

If you're solution focused, the loss of a client and subsequent business downturn gives you the opportunity to focus on prospecting for other, better clients. It isn't an excuse to slow down and become less active!

This advice is very different from what you might have heard from other people within the mental health field. "Talk about your problems and you'll feel better" has become so much of a cliché that it's even been a punch line on Seinfeld.[3]

There's one problem with that. No studies have conclusively shown that talking about or thinking about problems will naturally lead people to solutions.

It's the same as thinking about a broken leg and expecting the bone to heal itself quickly and cleanly. It isn't any more rational to do it on a figurative problem than it is to do it on a physical one. By immediately framing a problem in the solution framework and asking yourself to come up with one step you can take that can make things better—and doing it within sixty seconds—you're aligning your mind with powerful beneficial forces. And you will be taking useful actions before negative emotions can start to cycle you into a bigger and bigger hole.

You're literally manufacturing optimism and success.

The Big Why: It is totally normal to focus on excuses, things you cannot control, and your problems. The goal is to be *abnormal*, and to do so you must learn to vaccinate yourself against the three performance viruses: "The Trap of the Viable Excuse," "Focusing on What You Can't Control," and "Giving In to Problem-Centric Thought."

The Inversion Test: If you do not vaccinate yourself against excuse making, allowing your mind to focus on what you cannot control, and problem-centric thinking, you will be significantly less happy, less healthy, and less successful.

Act Now: Write down your three most common viable excuses. The act of recognizing the excuses you use causes your mind to be more sensitive to not using them in the future.

Here are some examples of the three most commonly used excuses from our clients to help get you started:

PRO ATHLETE

1. My competition makes a lot more money than I do—of course he's better than I am.
2. I'm not sure why but that ump has it out for me. I never get the calls with him.
3. As the game or season wears on, I sometimes catch myself thinking that I am wearing down and getting tired, and that is my excuse for giving less than 100 percent to my training and preparation.

FINANCIAL ADVISOR

1. My assistant continues to make mistakes. She often misses deadlines or says the wrong things to clients, and then I have to continually clean up the mess. That's why I can't get organized daily.
2. I have so much paperwork and my clients expect me to get it done. There just aren't enough hours in the day to get all of that stuff done and make my proactive contacts.
3. When the market is bad, there is nothing I can do to make things better.

continues

LAWYER

1. I am too busy making money to do any prospecting.
2. I am too busy making money to get home on time.
3. When the office calls, it is so important that I have to answer—even during family dinner time.

Once you've admitted to your excuses, it's time to start thinking of solutions. Take the time to do another exercise: think of one problem you have been worried about, but quickly come up with one simple step you can take that is solution-oriented. This exercise should take no longer than sixty seconds. Then, write down exactly when you will take that step. You will be on your way to a brighter future.

Epilogue
Inspiration and Beyond

Inspiration is a powerful thing.

Coach Wooden's father, Joshua, raised his children to live by two sets of simple rules. The first set dealt with integrity:

- Never lie.
- Never cheat.
- Never steal.

The second set dealt with adversity.

- Don't whine.
- Don't complain.
- Don't make excuses.

And when Coach Wooden graduated from the eighth grade, in 1924, his father gave him a printed card. On one side was an inspirational poem by the Reverend Henry van Dyke, a Presbyterian minister who wrote many popular stories and hymns in the early twentieth century. On the other side was a seven-point creed that included advice like "Make each day your masterpiece."

Wooden took the two sets of three rules and the advice on that card (which he carried with him in his pocket to the day he died in 2010) and used them every day in more than seventy years of coaching and mentoring.

The thousands of people Wooden touched were in turn inspired by Joshua Wooden's gesture nearly a hundred years ago. To this day, you can listen to the words of the all-time great players mentored by Wooden—Kareem Abdul-Jabbar, Bill Walton, Gail Goodrich—and hear Wooden's influence, down to the exact language he used with them in practice decades ago.[1]

————

Our goal in this book—and in every seminar we teach—is the same as the one Coach Wooden had for every practice he ran: we want you to leave a little better than you came in.

Here, we'd like to share five real success stories from families who embraced the concepts we teach and changed not just their lives but the lives of their children. In many ways, these families may be like yours. And their transformations didn't come from some kind of dramatic meteor strike from outer space or thunderbolt from the sky. It came from methodical, incremental improvement—and the determination to make those improvements stick.

You can do it, too.

THE LANGUAGE OF A LOSER

Marcus Lopez hadn't yet attended one of our classes, but he received one of our audio CDs from a financial advisor friend who had. Marcus listened to the CD so much that it actually got stuck in the slot in his car radio—so he ended up listening to it much more often than he had planned. He didn't realize just how often until he was driving back from a golf tournament that his ten-year-old son had played in.

His son had a tough round, and he spent the first part of the car ride talking about all of the problems with his game—everything from his clubs to the condition of the course to the fact that everybody in the tournament was a better player than he was.

When the ten-year-old took a breath, his five-year-old brother chimed in. "That's whining, complaining, and making excuses," he said. "You're speaking in the language of a loser."

That lesson became one that all of Marcus's family shared together on a regular basis. It led to a little game: When one of the kids heard something on television that sounded like whining, complaining, or making an excuse, they'd almost automatically point it out. Marcus would start the next sentence: "That's the language of a . . . ," and the kids would say, in unison, " . . . a loser, Dad."

Coach Wooden would have been pleased to learn that children were learning to adopt the "no excuse" mentality.

GRAPPLING WITH
THE MENTAL WORKOUT

Brian Blough is a very successful business owner from Georgia who attended one of our seminars and incorporated the Mental Workout into his routine the first day after the program finished. He had so much success with it that he shared the process with a number of other colleagues in his area—and with his sixteen-year-old son, who wrestles on the high school team.

In his second year on varsity, Brian's son had the ups and downs you would expect from a younger competitor. As he progressed through the season, his record hovered around .500. But as he got to the end of the season and started facing tougher competition, he began to wrestle much more conservatively.

After a conversation before one of his matches, Brian realized that his son was letting the prospect of competing against talented wrestlers get in his head. That night, he introduced him to the Mental Workout, and took him through all of the steps he had learned in our seminar. They created an identity statement, and his son began to visualize a highlight reel of success from his previous matches, and pictured in his mind's eye what he wanted his next match to look like.

In the next match, his son took the mat looking much calmer and more confident. A few weeks later, he wrestled extremely well in the sectional tournament—where he also advanced to make it into the state tournament. After a great showing in the state tournament, he's looking forward to a complete off-season to further develop his mental and physical skills—and to making an even longer run in next year's tournament.

BUILDING MENTAL TOUGHNESS

Rosey Hayett thought the principles he learned from Tom and Jason would be perfect to use in his role as a youth sports coach. Some of the most valuable material for the young athletes was on the subject of mental toughness.

Hayett's alpine ski racers faced some of the most daunting pressure of any youth athletes. Ski racing itself is a physically demanding sport that requires tremendous fitness and athleticism. The conditions are often brutal—cold weather, unfamiliar terrain, bad snow conditions.

As hard as that all is, the mental demands might even be tougher. The difference between first and fifth place is usually measured in hundredths of a second. One tiny mistake can blow up what was otherwise a great run. To compound the performance pressure, racers often have to go to the top of the slope and wait more than an hour to go down the hill, giving them plenty of time to think—and get nervous. A sound mental approach is absolutely crucial in the sport—especially for young athletes.

The team Hayett coached adopted Mental Workouts for each racer—the centering breaths, positive self-talk, and visualization helped to calm each of the skiers before their events and increased their confidence during runs. They also modified their practice routine to start treating training runs as if they were real, competitive ones—which helped them develop more tolerance for pressure.

By any measure, the tools were a success. On Hayett's team there were skiers from many small towns around northern New Mexico, and they regularly competed against larger, better-funded teams from higher population areas across three states. With the help of the mental workout, their team won the Southern Series championship four times in five seasons and produced a dozen Junior Olympic champions.

PRIORITIZING THE PROCESS

John Mark Brown is an Edward Jones advisor who went through one of our training seminars a few years ago. He started to see some great improvement in his business in the twelve months after the seminar, to the tune of a 19 percent increase. But it was the effect the training had on John's family life that proved to be the most valuable gain of all.

John's daughter Regan had been born four months premature and was diagnosed with cerebral palsy. She worked hard and pushed herself to lead the regular life of an elementary, junior high, and high school student, but she had her share of challenges. One day, about four months after John took the seminar, the superintendent of Regan's high school called. She asked what the family had been doing differently, because Regan's engagement and participation in her classes had gone way up.

John was stumped for a minute, then realized that the act of concentrating on the process of his business—the one rule he chose to hit hard after training—was spilling over into his family life, too. He was choosing to concentrate on the process of family time. Everybody in the Mark house was more engaged and working together, focusing on the process of growing and improving without worrying so much about the outcome or achieving perfection. Regan was feeding off that positive energy—with great results.

Regan graduated from high school with a B average and is now going to college.

FROM PERFECTION TO PERFORMANCE

Jeff Gayanski had always tried to motivate and push his kids the way he had been taught—to relentlessly attack until you got the results you wanted. It had worked for him. Jeff was a managing director for a Fortune 500 company, and he had found great success during his professional career by focusing harder and harder on getting those results.

But Jeff's family life wasn't keeping up with his professional life. He felt burned out with the relentlessness of work pressure. It was a phase that had come and gone before, but this time it seemed to be lasting much longer. And more importantly, Jeff's daughter was struggling, and he didn't know how to help her. None of his usual motivational tools were working.

Jeff was noticing some dramatic changes in his seven-year-old. She was obviously distressed about something. She was very emotional over small things, bursting into tears almost instantly over little frustrations. She was dealing with her anxiety by pulling her eyebrows out. Imagine how difficult it would be for a seven-year-old to have to go to school without eyebrows!

Doctors eventually diagnosed Jeff's daughter as having high anxiety, and said the family would need to learn how to deal with it the best they could. Jeff came to one of our seminars right about the time he was at his low point both professionally and personally. He was desperate, and he thought that if he could improve his work numbers, he could give himself some more breathing room at home.

It took a few days, but we showed him that he *wasn't* his results. He was his effort.

Jeff resolved to stop focusing on his numbers and to start concentrating on things he could control. He trained himself to answer three simple effort-based questions every day:

1. What three things did I do well today?
2. What one thing do I want to improve tomorrow?
3. What is one thing I can do differently right now that can help me make that improvement?

In the made-for-TV movie of Jeff's life, he would have answered those three questions on the first day, and everything would have solved itself immediately. Jeff lives in the real world, though, and it took a lot of determination—and some pain—to establish the new habit. Most days, he didn't want to bother to take the three minutes to answer the questions. But he doggedly did it, forcing himself to check off the box every day.

Jeff started noticing how much less anxiety he felt when he answered the questions. Then, he started to see an uptick in his results—ironically enough, right when he committed to not worrying about them. More importantly, the benefits began to seep into his home life. Jeff wasn't coming home tired and stressed out.

His wife and kids now enjoyed the time they had together each night. The more Jeff talked about the process he had learned in class, the more his wife wanted to know about it. Maybe the new process could help their family, and do something for their daughter. Maybe this new definition of success could reduce some of the frustration she was feeling. They decided to try. They started a new ritual. Every night, at dinner as a family, they decided to go around the table and identify one thing each did well that day.

Shockingly, Jeff's daughter started to respond. This one simple change helped her stop focusing so much on all the negative things in life and to be more aware of the good. Her stress level went way down, and her smile reappeared. In addition, she began using centering breaths to battle anxiety when she felt it coming on. A few months later, she went back to school for the first time in many years with all of her eyebrows intact.

Her confidence grew to the point where she even started joining extracurricular activities. At the low point, she never would have considered playing on a team, because of the fear she wouldn't be able to handle the pressure. Last fall, she hit nine service winners in a row to win the title for her volleyball team. In more ways than one, she's a hero.

KNOWING SOMETHING DOES NOTHING. DOING SOMETHING DOES

The success stories we've told in this chapter (and in this book) all have one thing in common. The central people in them are doers. If the commitment to doing isn't there, success doesn't exist.

It's up to you to change the lens through which you see the world. Instead of telling yourself you aren't special enough to get all the things you want in life, start telling yourself *I deserve it*—and then start deserving it by taking action!

PICK ONE . . . AND WE MEAN IT

Our main priority for this book has been to give you a variety of techniques you can use to increase your success—and to give you permission to choose only one of those techniques to attack at a time.

Ritualizing one change will bring you much more success than if you try to bite off everything at once—just like taking the entire bottle of aspirin isn't the right solution for muscle pain. Remember, done is better than perfect.

We can already read the minds of some of you looking over this paragraph right now. The whole concept of choosing just one thing doesn't apply to you, right? You're too advanced, too smart, and too special. It's great to have that kind of self-belief, and often, it's something you can use. But in this case, you're wrong.

In almost twenty years of working with some of the most successful and talented people in the world, we've seen the power and the value of focusing on one improvement at a time—no matter what kind of physical and mental horsepower you bring to the table.

Once you've nailed your one improvement for three consecutive months (and 90 percent completion is how we define "nailing it"), you're ready to move on to the next challenge. By doing it this way, you're actually speeding up the growth process. It won't all happen overnight, but your improvement will be steady, and it'll be lasting.

Play Hard, Play Smart

Everything we've been talking about in this book has been designed to give you the information you need and the motivation to use it. Taken together, those two things produce the single most important factor in human performance—confidence.

If you watch any sport on television, you've certainly heard "confidence" used as a catchphrase, or shorthand, for being "in the groove." "He's playing with a lot of confidence," or, "She really needs to make this shot to get some confidence back," are things announcers say all the time. And it's certainly true that confidence is what often separates one athlete from another. Two athletes may both have world-class physical skill, but the one who has just a little more of that mental and emotional intangible is the one who has the better chance of success. So you probably won't be surprised to hear that confidence is just as big of a factor in everyday life, for everyday people, as it is in NCAA basketball games, NASCAR races, or Olympic sprints. Confidence matters just as much for you and me as it does for Lebron James, Jordan Spieth, or Ronda Rousey.

Think about the times in your life when you've had a lot of confidence—and when you've had less of it. And think about how easy it is to *lose* confidence.

It's happened to all of us. You're feeling great about work, but then you run into a bad manager who puts you into a sidespin. Or things are running smoothly at work and one of your children runs into a problem that is complicated and hard to solve.

It happens. Life is how you deal with it when it does.

Confidence isn't some kind of magic trick. It isn't something people are automatically born with. It's something you can learn, and something you can practice. It's what we've been teaching folks in dozens of training seminars all over the country.

If you apply even just one of the lessons from this book—and choose wisely—you're going to set up your own process for making your confidence grow.

As a reminder, we want to leave you with a few guidelines to help keep you on that confidence track.

1. Choose wisely. Your mind is like a powerful fire hose. Don't dilute the strength by splitting the stream and aiming at a bunch of different fires. Pick one concept at a time and fully acknowledge the limits of channel capacity.

2. Nail it—90 percent of the time. Once you've chosen, give it time to work and become habit. For the next three months, concentrate on that one concept and make it second nature.

3. Improve, not perfect. If you expect perfection in anything—yourself, your spouse, your kids—you're setting yourself—or them—up for failure and disappointment. First, understand that just the act of deciding to make a change and trying to improve sets you apart from most people. Benjamin Franklin said it first, and he was paraphrased by General George S. Patton: "Most people die at a very early age, only to be buried 40 or 50 years later." Congratulate yourself for taking the initiative, and keep pushing for improvement—not perfection.

4. Evaluate smartly. When you do improve, recognize it. Don't be critical about the size or speed of improvement. Congratulate yourself, then write down what you want to continue to improve. Making the effort is winning in and of itself.

5. Repetition, repetition, repetition, repetition. . . . Mastery only comes from effort and repetition. You wouldn't expect your five-year-old to be able to tie her shoes the first time. In the words of the Zen master Suzuki, if you lose the spirit of repetition, your practice will become difficult. This was one of the absolute cornerstones of Coach Wooden's teaching.[2]

6. Be your own best cheerleader. Friends, family, loved ones, and colleagues might recognize the things you're trying to improve, and they might not. It's up to you to reinforce your own positive feelings. When you make progress, don't hesitate to celebrate it. You'll build a feedback loop that recruits your mind toward the next reward.

The Big Why: Life is hard and most people are overwhelmed. It's important to remember that you can do it. You have the power to improve. When you take action on your one thing, you will deserve the success you experience.

The Inversion Test: People who try to take action on too many things become overwhelmed to a point of inaction. People who try to take action on one thing become energized to a point of action.

Act Now: Pick one thing from the list of chapters to attack. Evaluate yourself weekly on your completion rate. Make it a goal to nail your one thing each week at 90 percent or better.

Chapter 1: Organize Tomorrow Today

ACTION TOOL: Identify daily your "3 Most Important / 1 Must."

Chapter 2: Choose Wisely

ACTION TOOL: Every day, no matter what, take *action* on your "1 Must."

Chapter 3: Maximize Your Time

ACTION TOOL: Choose one of the three time-maximization tools described in the chapter and commit to following it

continues

("Attack the Open Space," "Prioritize the Priorities," "Trim the Fat").

Chapter 4: Win Your Fight-Thrus

ACTION TOOL: Win fight-thrus by asking yourself two questions: How will I feel if I win the fight-thru? How will I feel if I lose it?

Chapter 5: Evaluate Correctly

ACTION TOOL: Complete Success Logs a minimum of three times weekly.

Chapter 6: Learn How to Talk to Yourself

ACTION TOOL: Complete Mental Workouts a minimum of three times weekly.

Chapter 7: Learn How to Talk with Others

ACTION TOOL: Before meetings and presentations, spend three minutes three times daily for three days mentally rehearsing what you will say and how you will say it.

Chapter 8: Become Abnormal

ACTION TOOL: Identify the one "virus" that is most affecting you, and take the action now to vaccinate yourself.

Here is how some of our clients tackled this assignment:

PRO ATHLETE

I am going to work on choosing wisely. I feel like there are actually two steps to this goal. First I am going to commit each and every day, no matter what, to complete my "1 Must." If I am going to finish my career strong, this has to be done. The other side of it for me is that I am going to do a better job of choosing wisely what I commit to. I am always telling people that I will do this or that without really giving much thought to whether or not I will actually follow through. I am going to really work on only saying things that I fully intend on following through with. I will choose more wisely.

FINANCIAL ADVISOR

There is no doubt what I need to choose to focus on. I need to get organized. I am going to attempt every day to identify my "3 Most Important / 1 Must." The rule I am setting up for myself is that before I am allowed to take my first bite of lunch I will spend a few minutes getting organized for tomorrow. To help with accountability, I am going to ask my assistant to come in and remind/ask me if I have

continues

completed my OTT before she takes her first bite of lunch each day.

PHYSICIAN

The one thing I am going to commit to moving forward is beating the "no excuse" virus. I am keenly aware that my one "go-to" excuse has been "I am too busy making money." This excuse has caused me for years to become stagnant. I don't read anymore, and that used to be a big part of making personal improvement. The worst part is I hide behind that excuse when it comes to being a good husband and father. I am embarrassed and heartbroken that I have allowed this to go on for so long, but I am committing to not using that excuse any longer.

We have one last thing to say. Be relentless about improvement; your progress has no limits!

Notes

INTRODUCTION

1. Dr. George Miller outlined the amount of information the human brain could process and retain at any given time in "The Magical Number Seven, Plus or Minus Two: Some Limits on Our Ability to Process Information," originally published in *Psychological Review* 63, no. 2 (1956).

2. "The Lollapalooza Effect" was coined by Charlie Munger in a June 1995 speech to the Harvard Law School.

CHAPTER 1

1. "The noise of the urgency creates an illusion of importance." Steven R. Covey, *The 7 Habits of Highly Effective People: Powerful Lessons in Personal Change* (New York: Simon and Schuster, 2013).

2. "Taking notes on laptops rather than in longhand is increasingly common. Many researchers have suggested that laptop note taking is less effective than longhand note taking for learning. Prior studies have primarily focused on students' capacity for multitasking and distraction when using laptops. The present research suggests

that even when laptops are used solely to take notes, they may still be impairing learning because their use results in shallower processing. In three studies, we found that students who took notes on laptops performed worse on conceptual questions than students who took notes longhand. We show that whereas taking more notes can be beneficial, laptop note takers' tendency to transcribe lectures verbatim rather than processing information and reframing it in their own words is detrimental to learning." Abstract from Pam A. Mueller and Daniel M. Oppenheimer, "The Pen Is Mightier Than the Keyboard: Advantages of Longhand over Laptop Note Taking," *Psychological Science,* April 23, 2014.

3. "Do Written Goals Really Make a Difference?," on a study by Dr. Gail Matthews, Dominican University, UGM Consulting, August 26, 2011, www.ugmconsulting.com/Do%20written%20goals%20really%20make%20a%20difference%20UGM%20Briefing%2026%20Aug%202011.pdf.

4. A concise description of and previous research about behavioral inertia appears in Raymond B. Huey, Paul E. Hertz, and B. Sinervo, "Behavioral Drive vs. Behavioral Inertia in Evolution: A Null Model Approach," *American Naturalist,* March 2003. B. F. Skinner's research was called "quantitative behavioral analysis."

5. Bluma Zeigarnik's research on "the influence of tension in the achievement of memory" originally appeared in a paper called "On Finished and Unfinished Tasks," *Psychologische Forschung,* 1927. Twenty years later, Kurt Lewin, one of Bluma Zeigarnik's earliest mentors, expanded on the concept of task-specific tension in his research; see his "Concept, Method and Reality in Social Science: Social Equilibria and Social Change," *Frontiers in Group Dynamics* 1, no. 1 (1947).

6. "The 19th century geometrist Jacobi once said that one should always try to invert every geometrical theory. But his advice applies much more widely! Choose any class of relational frames and you can study its valid modal axiom." Johan van Bethem, "Man Mass Immer

Umkehren," Institute for Logic, Language and Computation, January 2007.

CHAPTER 2

1. "Einstein said there are five ascending levels of intelligence: smart, intelligent, brilliant, genius and simple." "Understanding Circle of Competence and Knowing the Edge of Your Competency," *Forbes*, GuruFocus, January 2, 2015.

CHAPTER 3

1. Mike Berardino, "Mike Tyson Explains One of His Most Famous Quotes," *Sun-Sentinel* (Florida), November 9, 2012.

CHAPTER 4

1. Dr. Maxwell Maltz's original book, *Psycho-Cybernetics*, was published in 1960 by Prentice-Hall. It has been updated and republished many times since.

2. "How Long Does It Take to Form a Habit?," article published by the University College London in the UCL News website about research performed by UCL's Phillippa Lally and the Cancer Research UK Health Behaviour Research Centre, August 4, 2009, https://www.ucl.ac.uk/news/news-articles/0908/09080401.

HALFTIME

1. Anne Kathrin Barbeck and Thomas Neumann from Westfalische Wilhelms-Universitat Munster gave an extensive description of Dr. Jean Pol-Martin's research in their paper "Lernen durch Lehren (LdL) in Theory and Practice," for the seminar *Learner-Centered Approaches*, Wintersemester 2005/2006.

CHAPTER 5

1. Dr. Norman Doidge, *The Brain That Changes Itself: Stories of Personal Triumph from the Frontiers of Brain Science* (New York: James H. Silberman Books, 2007).

CHAPTER 6

1. Maxwell Maltz, *Psycho-Cybernetics* (Upper Saddle River, NJ: Prentice-Hall, 1960).

2. The quotation, in context, reads: "The human mind is like a fertile ground where seeds are continually being planted. The seeds are opinions, ideas, and concepts. You plant a seed, a thought, and it grows. The word is like a seed, and a human mind is so fertile!" Don Miguel Ruiz, *The Four Agreements: A Practical Guide to Personal Freedom* (San Rafael, CA: Amber-Allen Publishing, 1997).

CHAPTER 7

1. Steve Jobs's presenting skills were detailed extensively by Marcus Wohlsen in "The Apple Watch Is Steve Jobs' iPod Launch All Over Again," *WIRED*, September 10, 2014, and by Carmine Gallo in "11 Presentation Lessons You Can Still Learn from Steve Jobs," Forbes.com, October 4, 2012.

CHAPTER 8

1. David K. Randall, "The Day the Stocks Bottomed Out," *Forbes*, March 8, 2010, recounted the 2009 cratering of the stock market.

2. Gene Wojciechowski recounted the pivotal moment in the 2011 World Series in "Game 6 Defines What Baseball History Looks Like," ESPN.com, October 28, 2011, http://sports.espn .go.com/espn/columns/story?page=wojciechowski-111027.

3. In the *Seinfeld* episode "The Engagement," 1995, Kramer says, "What are you thinking about, Jerry? Marriage? Family? They're prisons! Man-made prisons. You're doing time. You get up in the morning, she's there. You go to sleep at night? She's there. It's like you gotta ask permission to go to the bathroom. 'Is it all right if I go to the bathroom now?' And you can forget about watching TV while you're eating. . . . You know why? Because it's dinnertime. And you know what you do at dinner? You talk about your day."

EPILOGUE

1. Joshua Wooden, "Timeless Wisdom Creed Cards," reproduced for the John Wooden Course, available at woodencourse.com.

2. Suzuki said, "If you lose the spirit of repetition, your practice will become quite difficult." Shunryu Suzuki, *Zen Mind, Beginner's Mind* (Boston: Shambhala, 2011).

About the Authors

Dr. Jason Selk is one of the premier performance coaches in the United States. His clients include Olympians and professional athletes in Major League Baseball, the NFL, the NBA, the NHL, and NASCAR, along with Fortune 500 executives and organizations such as Northwestern Mutual and Edward Jones. As the director of mental training for Major League Baseball's St. Louis Cardinals, Dr. Selk helped the team win two World Series championships, in 2006 and 2011. He previously wrote two best-selling books, *10-Minute Toughness* and *Executive Toughness;* is a regular contributor to ESPN, *Inc.,* and *Forbes;* and has been featured in *USA Today, Men's Health, Muscle & Fitness,* and *Self.* He lives outside St. Louis, Missouri. You can find him at JasonSelk.com.

Tom Bartow left a successful career as a college basketball coach to become one of the top financial advisors at Edward Jones. Tom applied many of the concepts he had learned from John Wooden, the famed basketball coach at UCLA, to create and develop an advanced training program for higher-level advisors at the firm. In June 1999, the American Funds Group offered Tom a unique position: one of his responsibilities was to work with American Funds distributors across the nation to increase the skill set of the entire sales organization. Tom's insights immediately proved to be highly beneficial to investors and advisors. From 2002 to 2009, Coach Wooden and Tom delivered a one-two punch for the American Funds Advisor Forums. Their friendship was such that Tom was invited to join Coach Wooden at the White House for Coach Wooden's acceptance of the Medal of Freedom. Coach Wooden said of Tom, "You are something else."

Tom Bartow and Dr. Jason Selk have become the best of friends and have worked together to bring peak performance techniques from the world of professional athletic competition to the corporate world.

Matthew Rudy has authored or coauthored twenty-three golf, business, and travel books, including titles with Hank Haney, Dr. Michael Lardon, Dave Stockton, and Johnny Miller. He is a senior writer at *Golf Digest*, where he has produced more than twenty-five cover stories since 1999. He lives in Bridgeport, Connecticut. You can find him at MatthewRudy.net, or on Twitter at @RudyWriter.

When you have your own breakthrough with the help of one of the rules in this book, we want to hear about it. Email jason@jasonselk.com. We'll use the best stories as case studies to help motivate the students that come behind you.

For more information on Organize Tomorrow Today classes and seminars in your area, or to inquire about scheduling them, go to Jasonselk.com.

Index